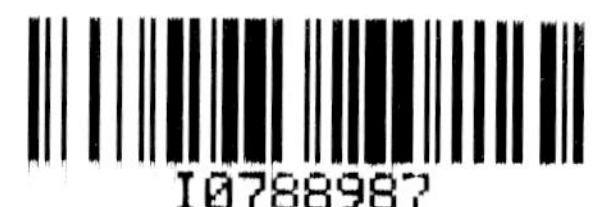

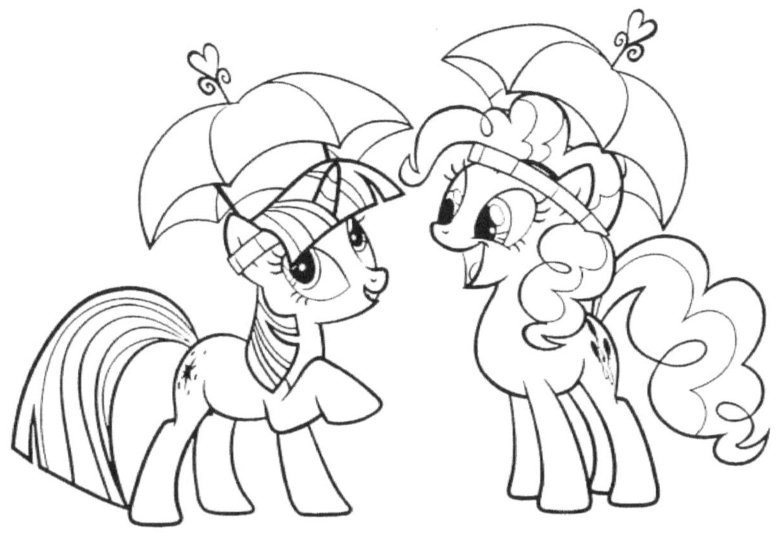

This Coloring Book Belongs To :

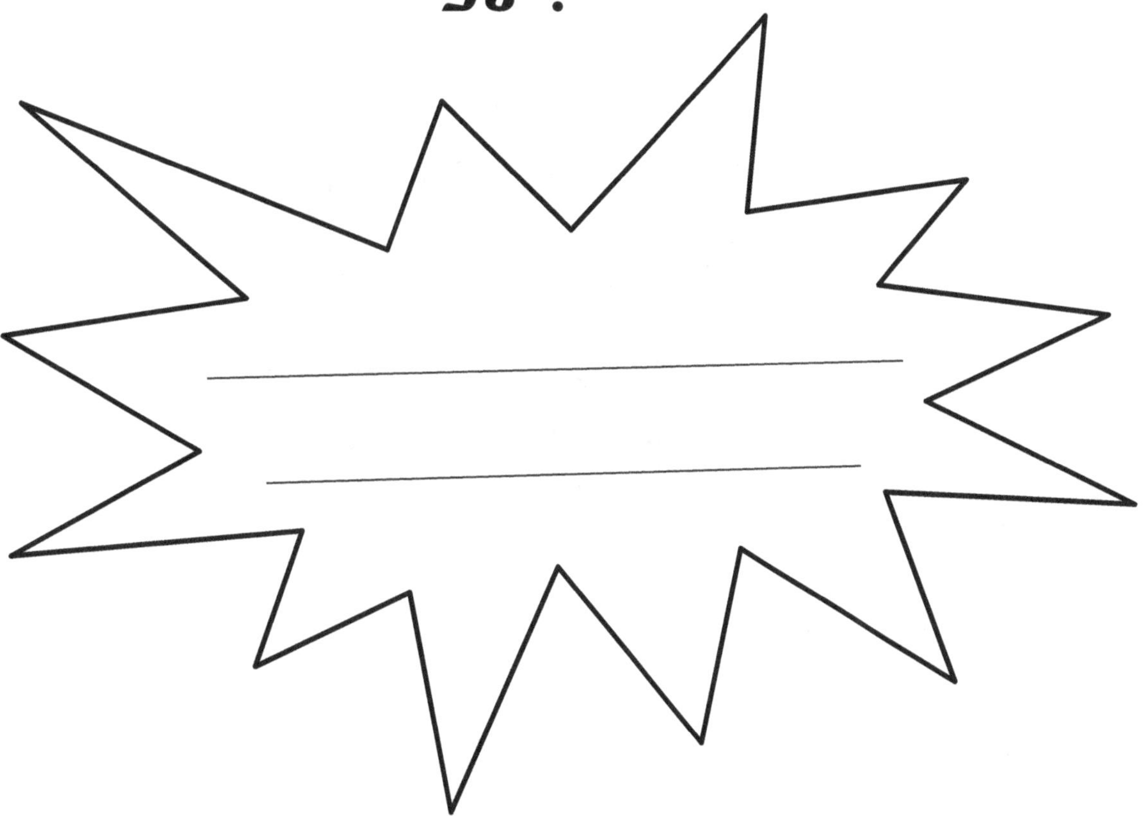

ENJOY ! 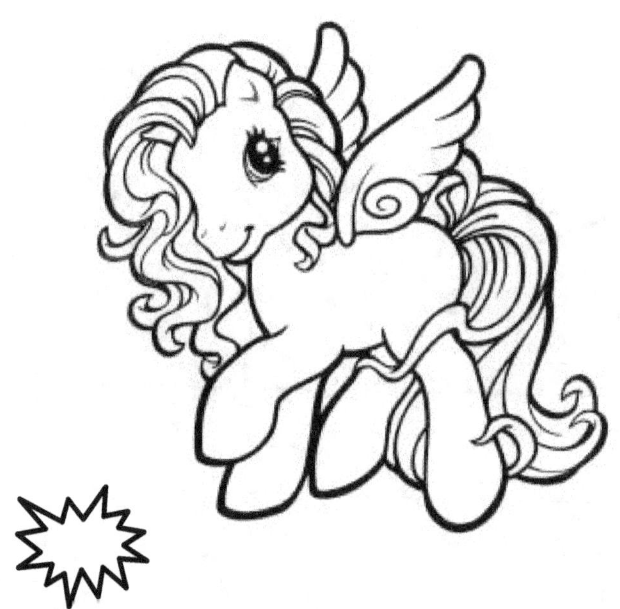

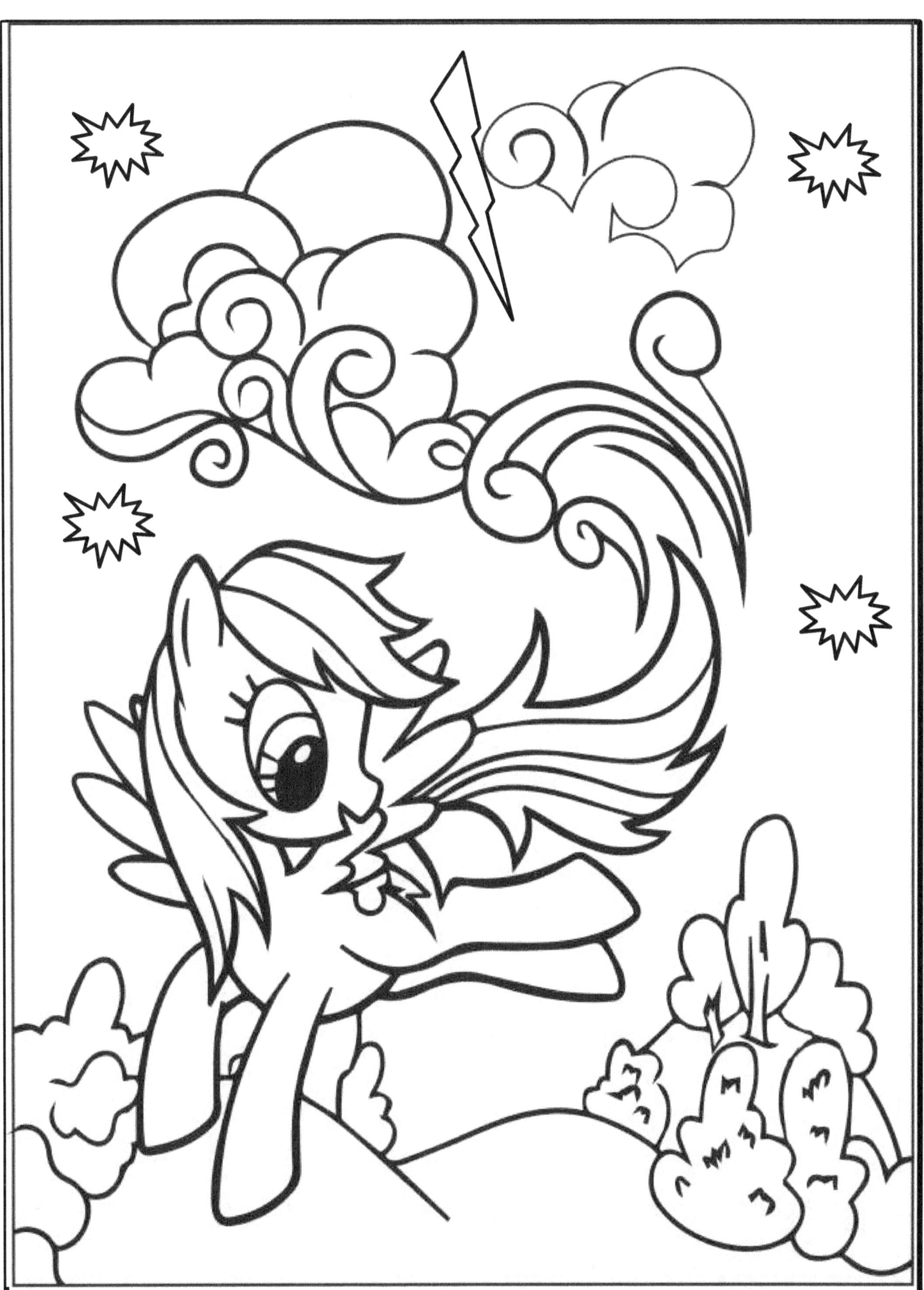

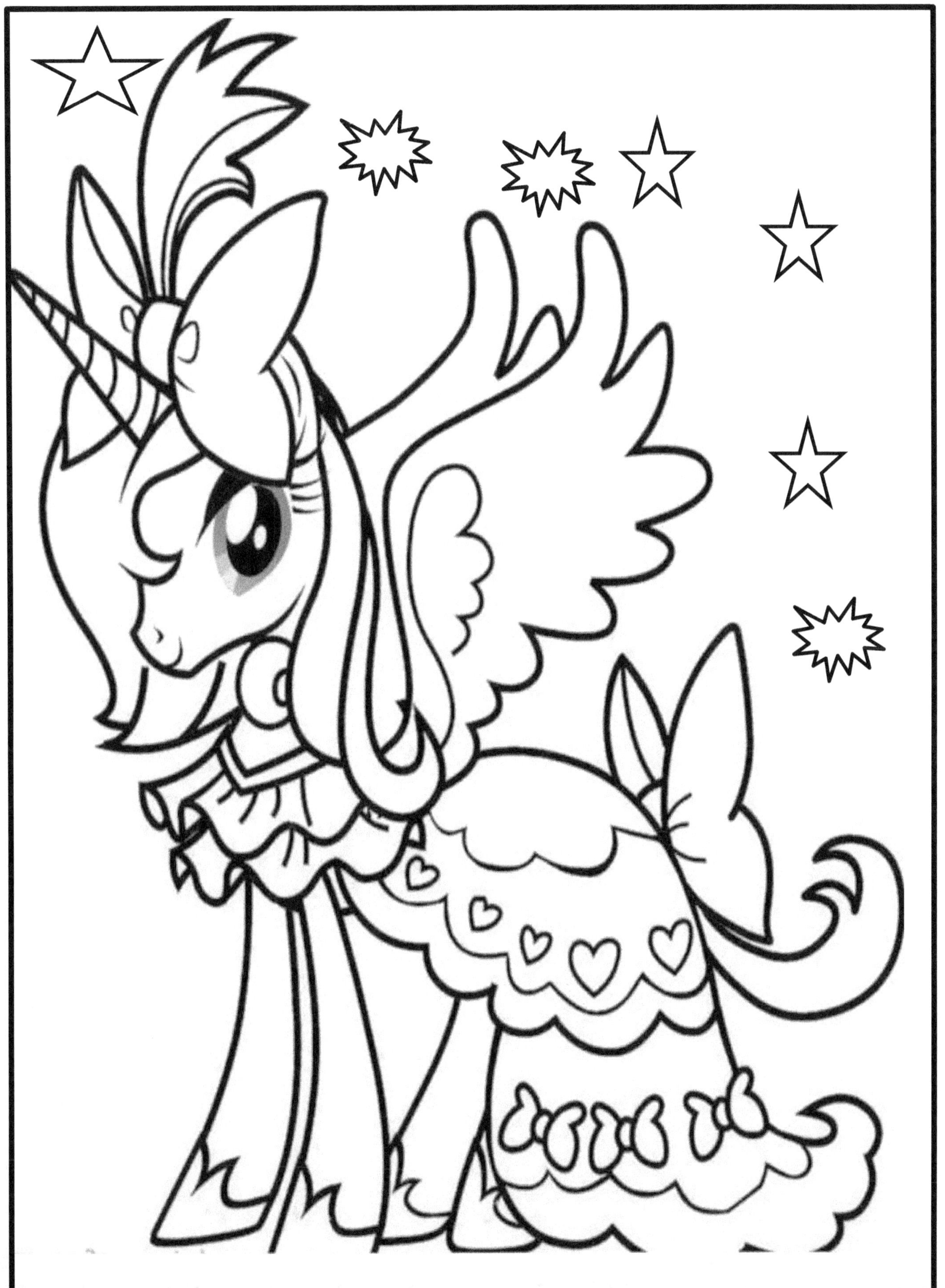

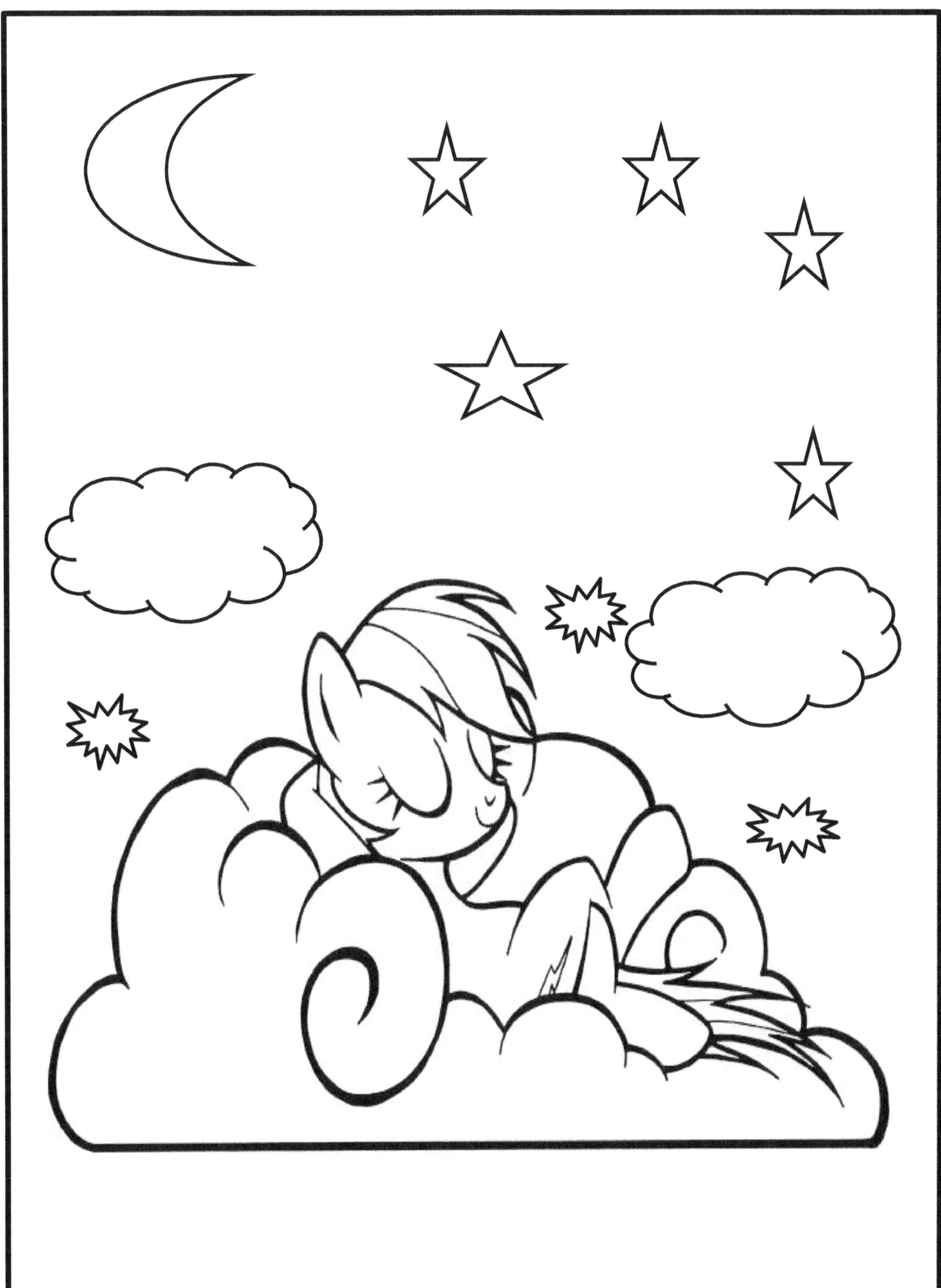

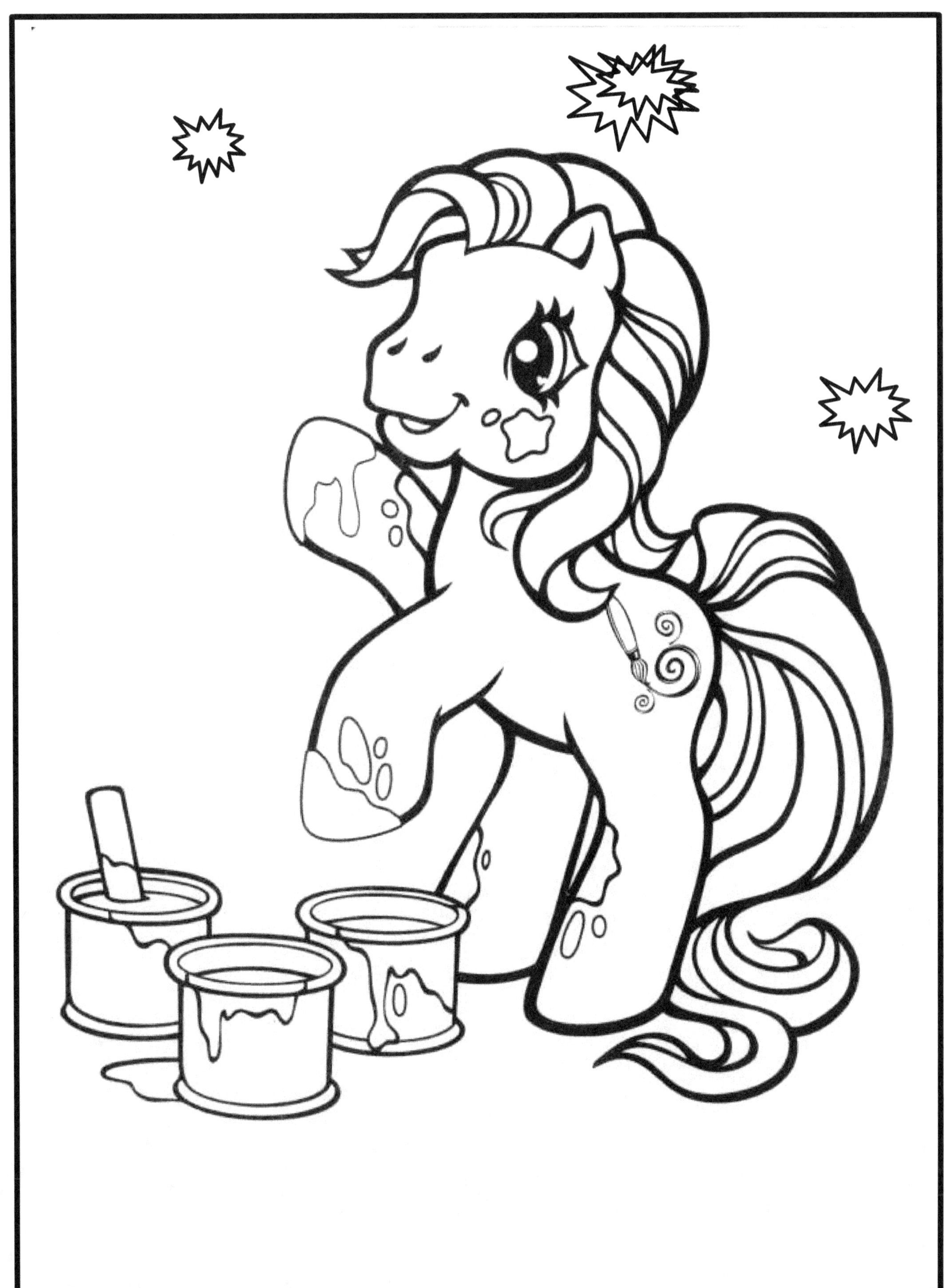

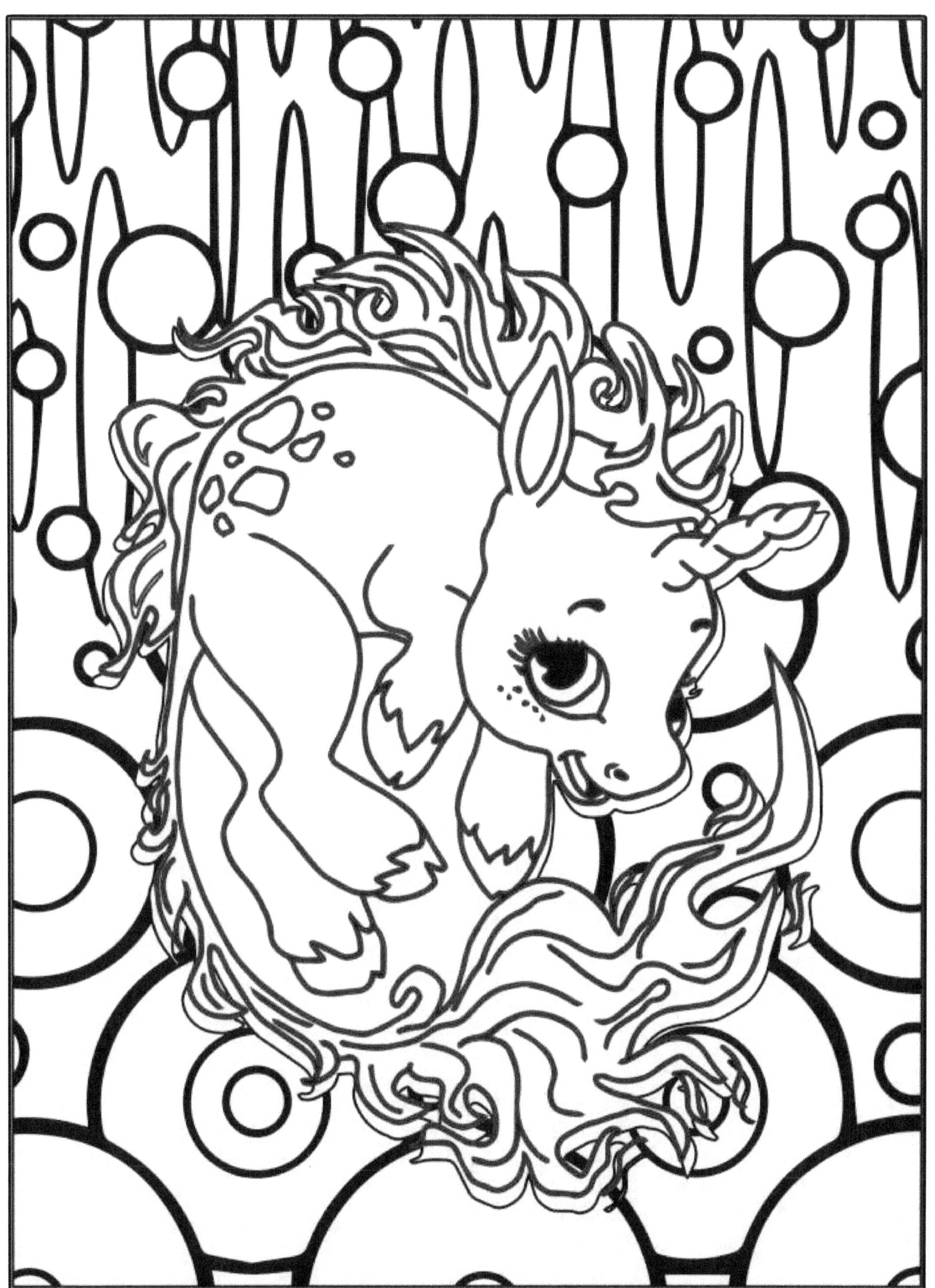

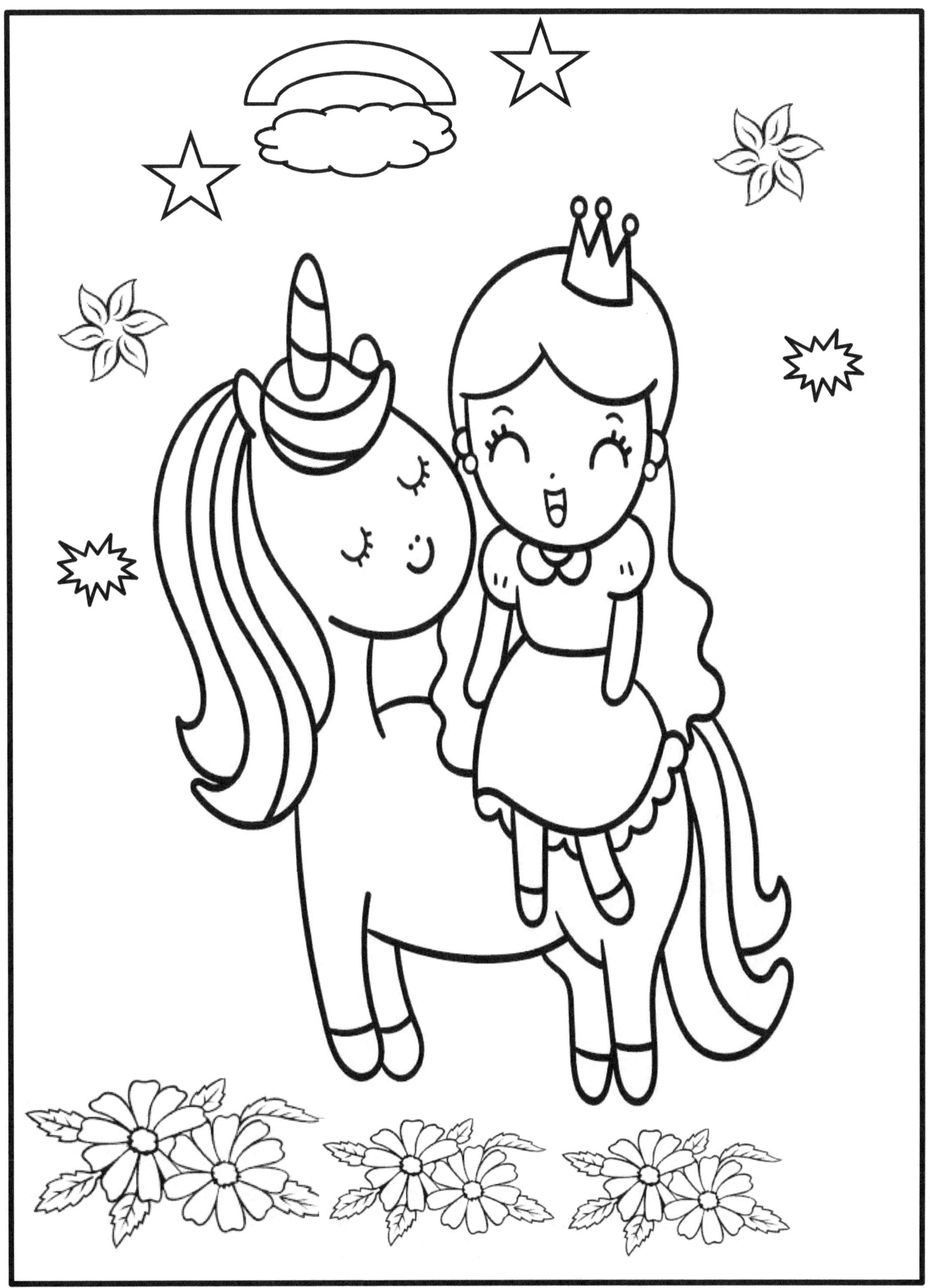

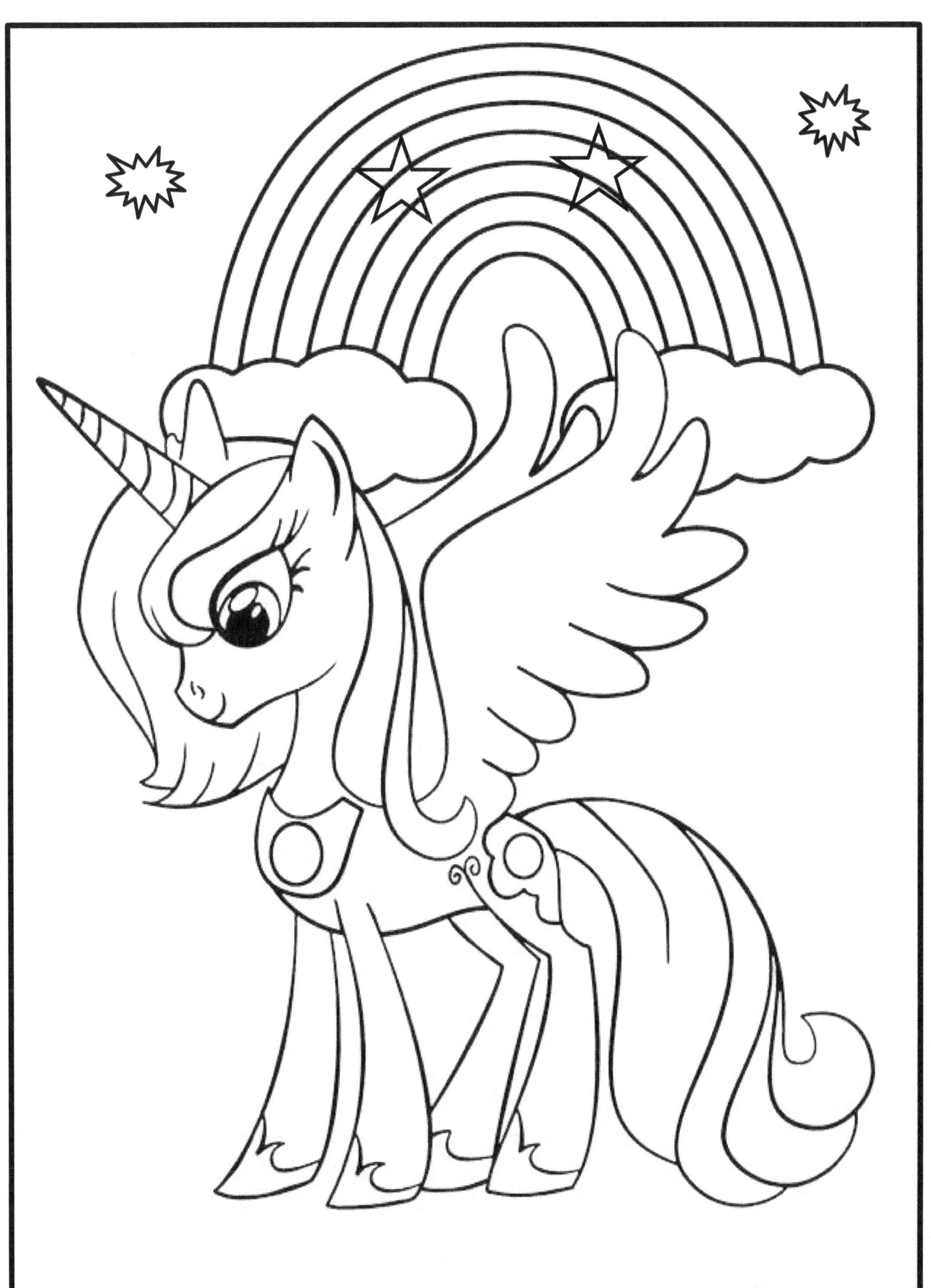

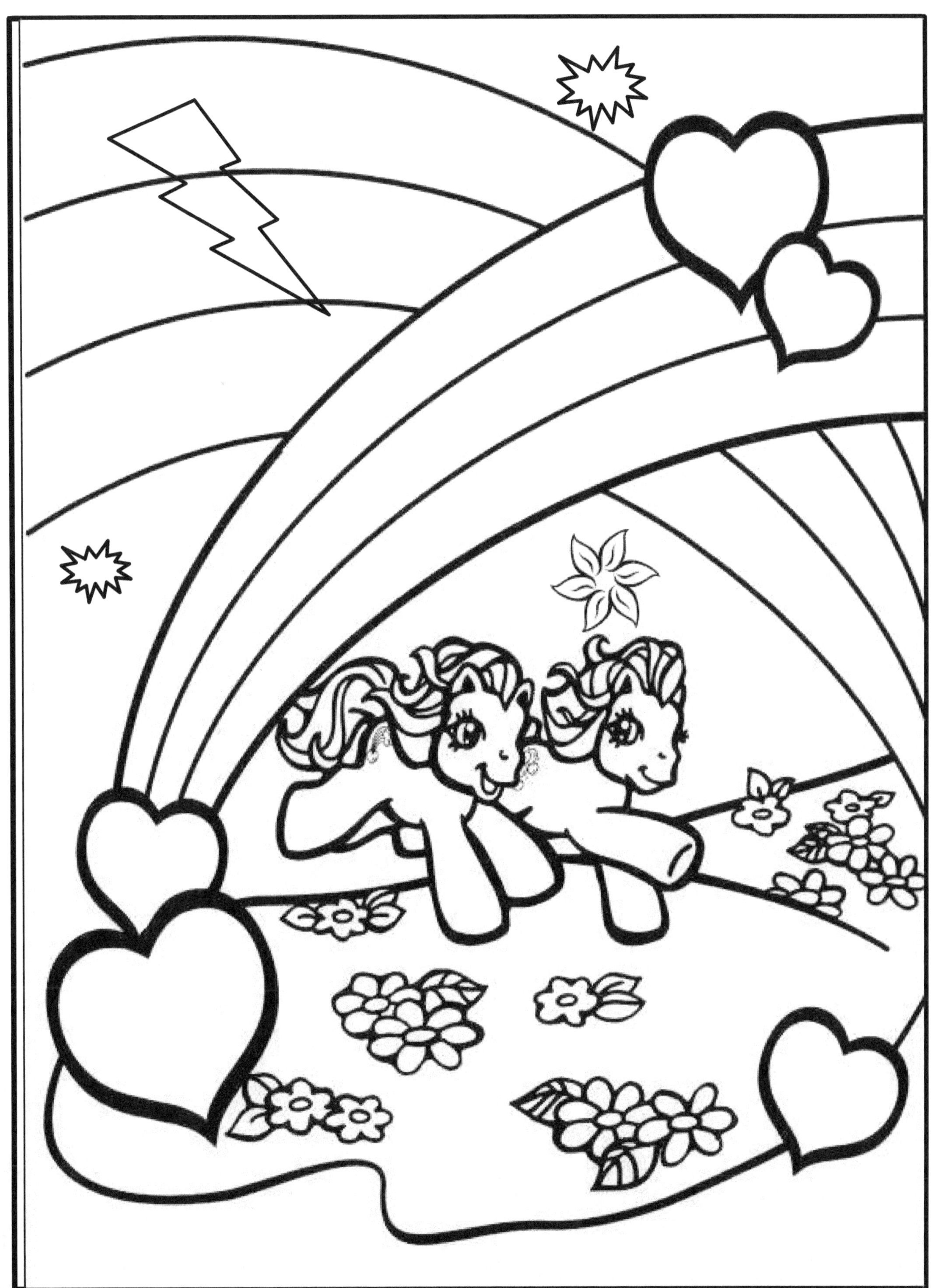

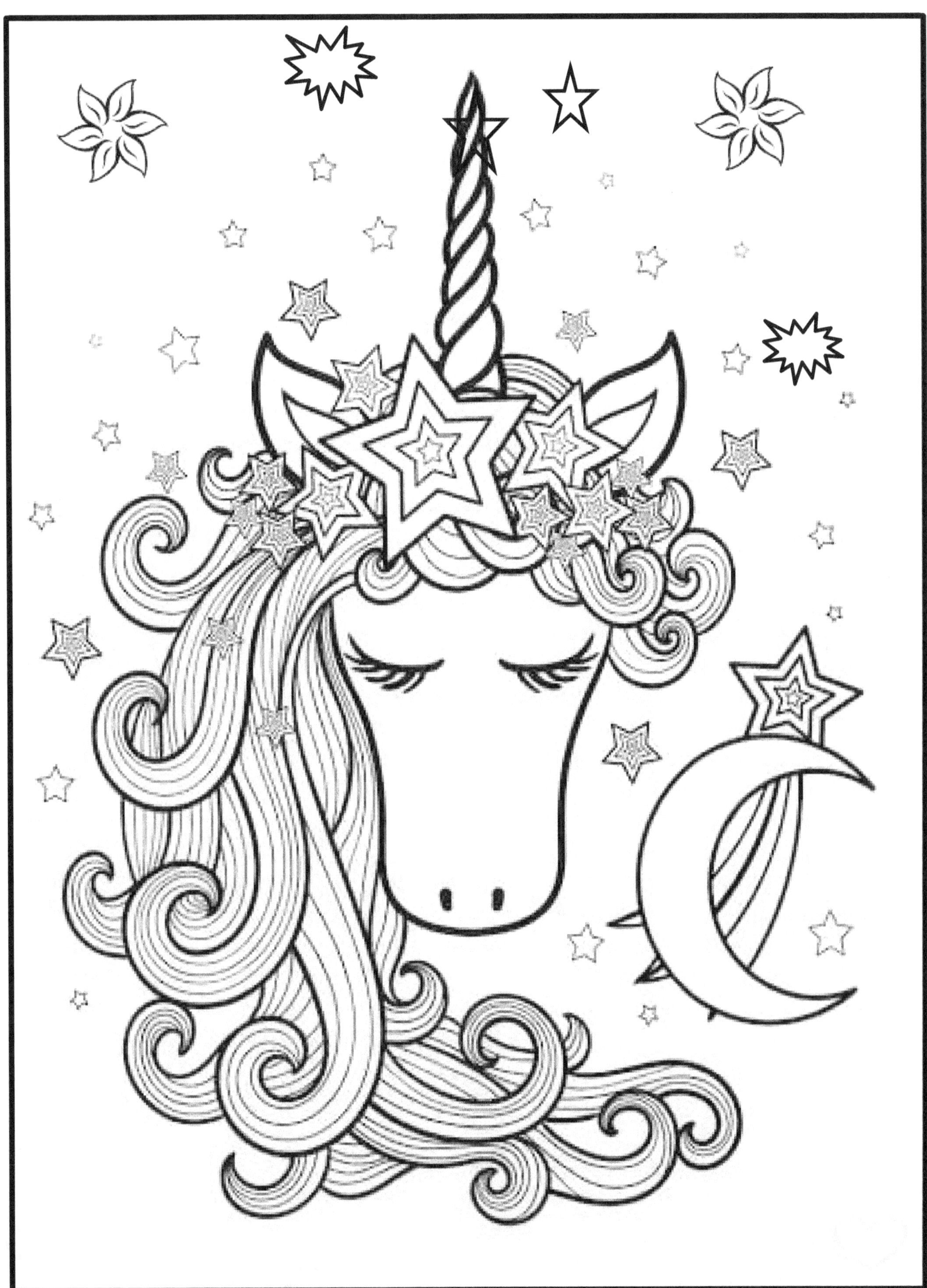

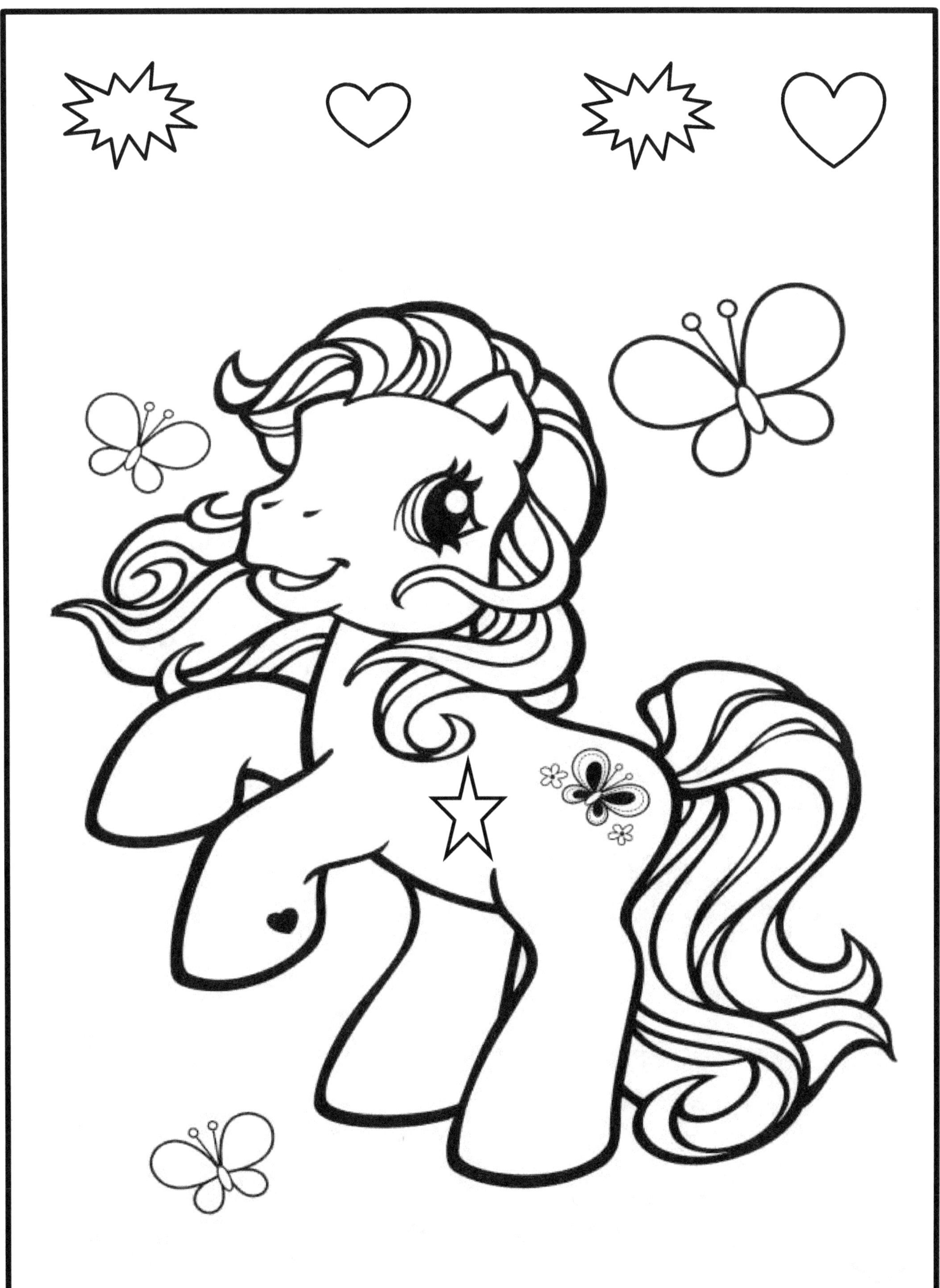

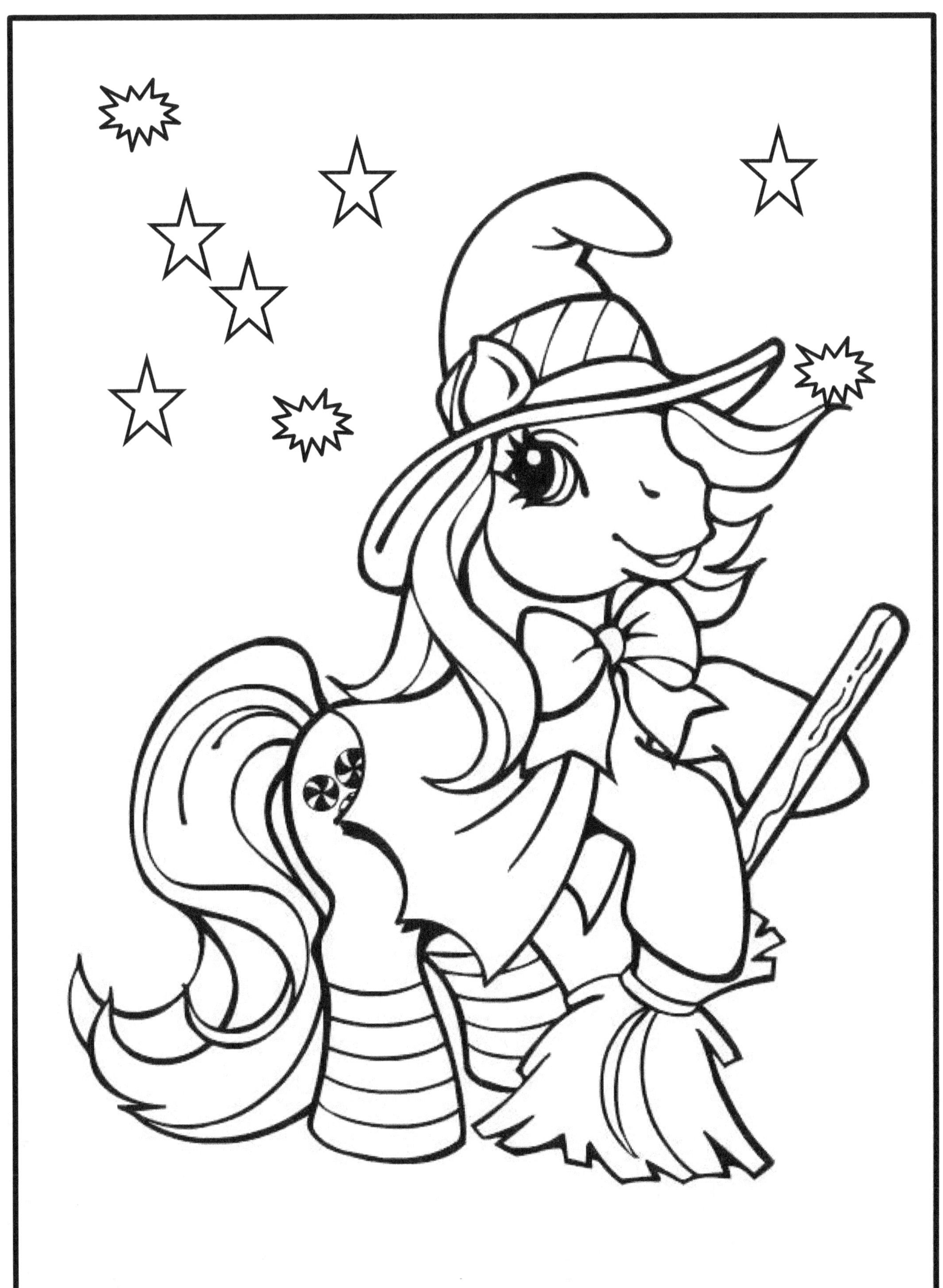

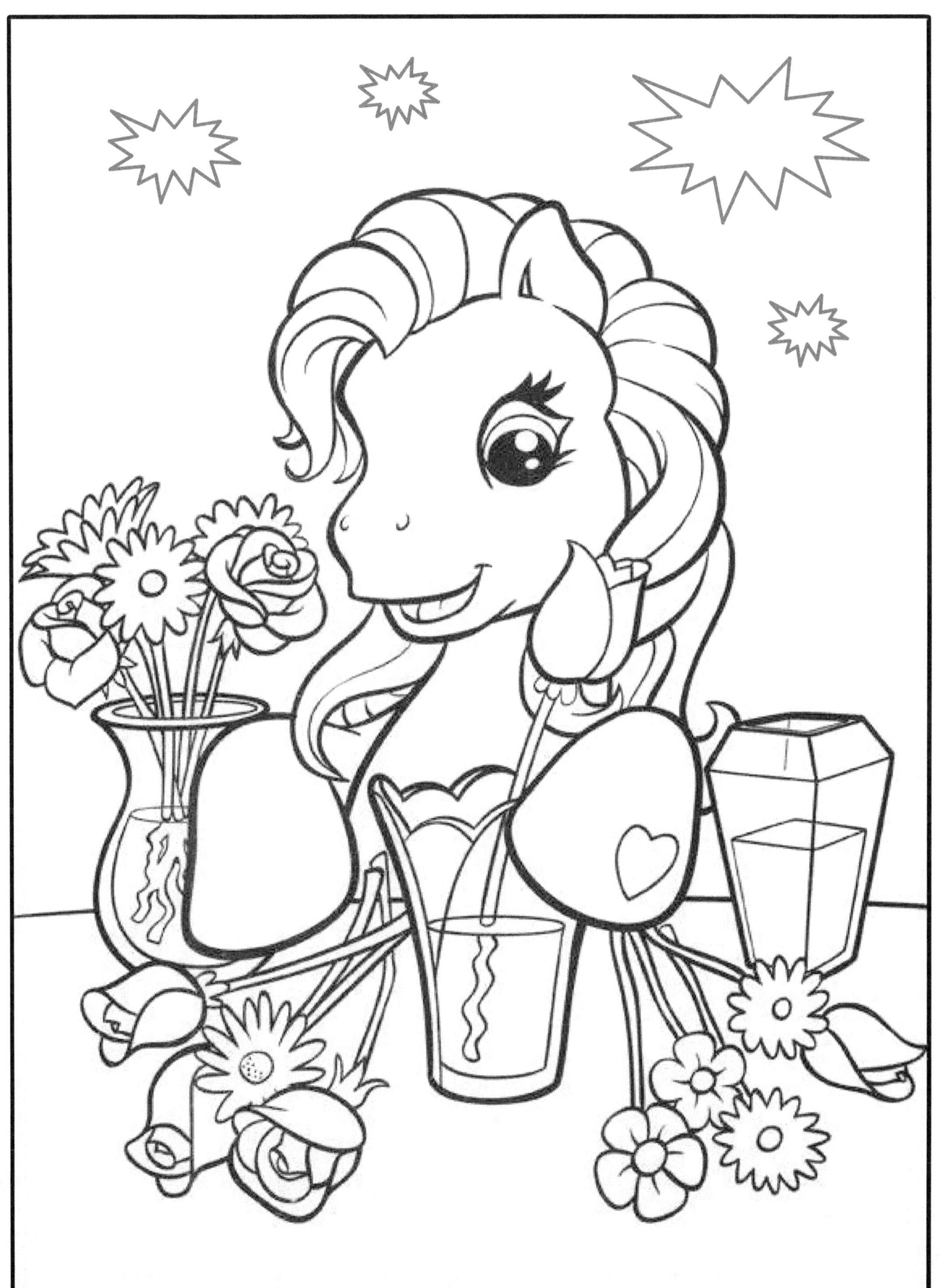

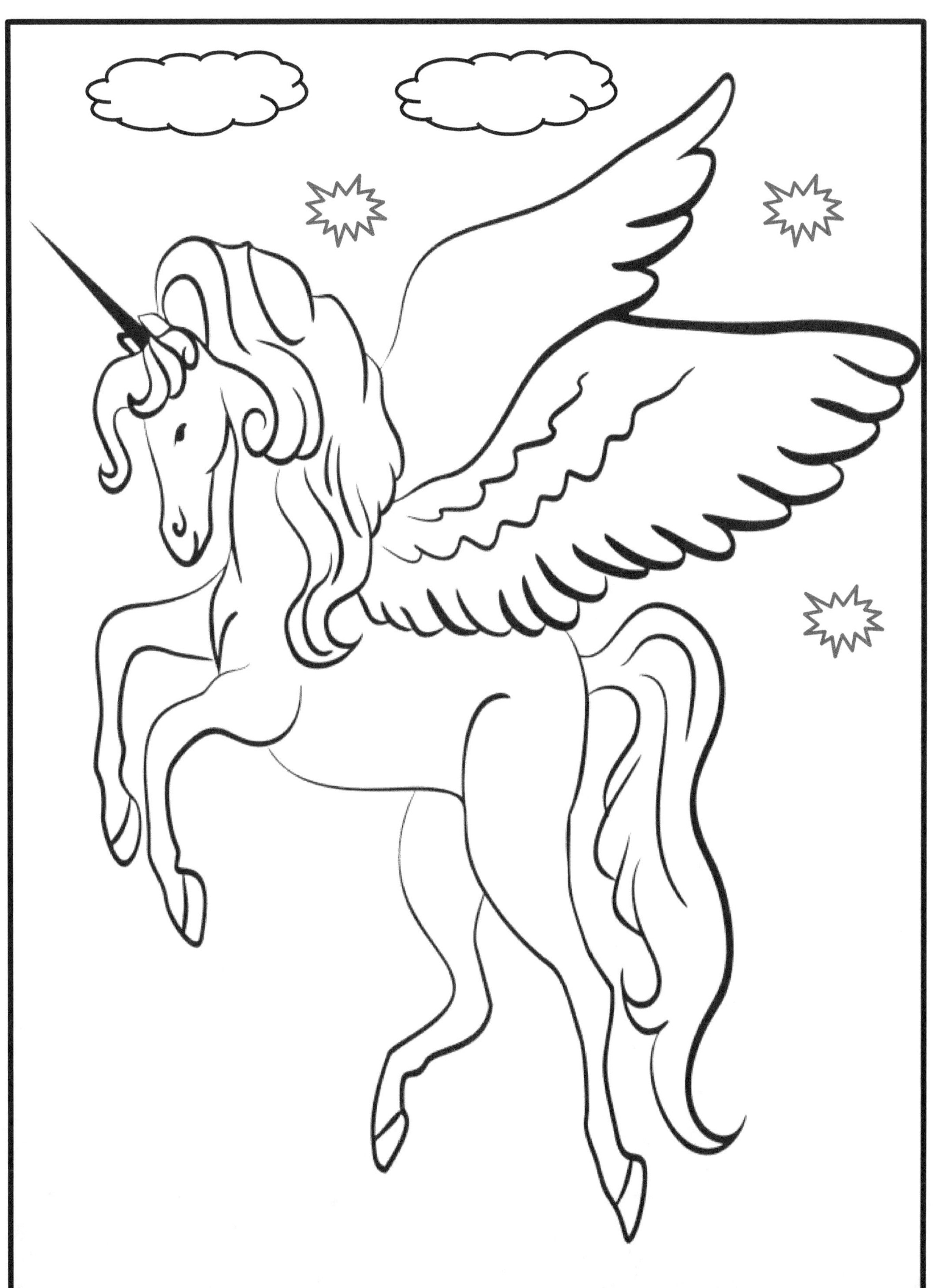

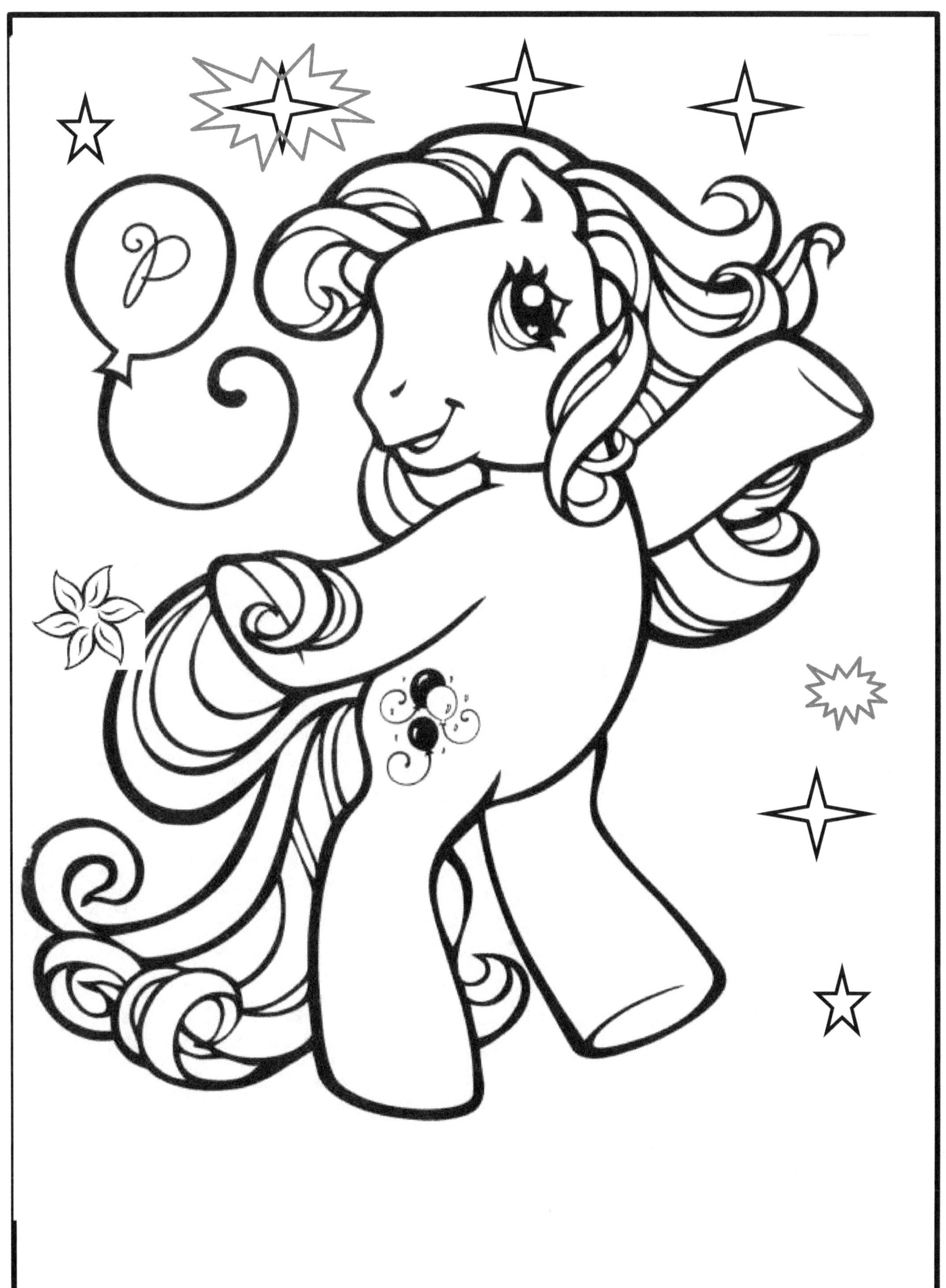
P

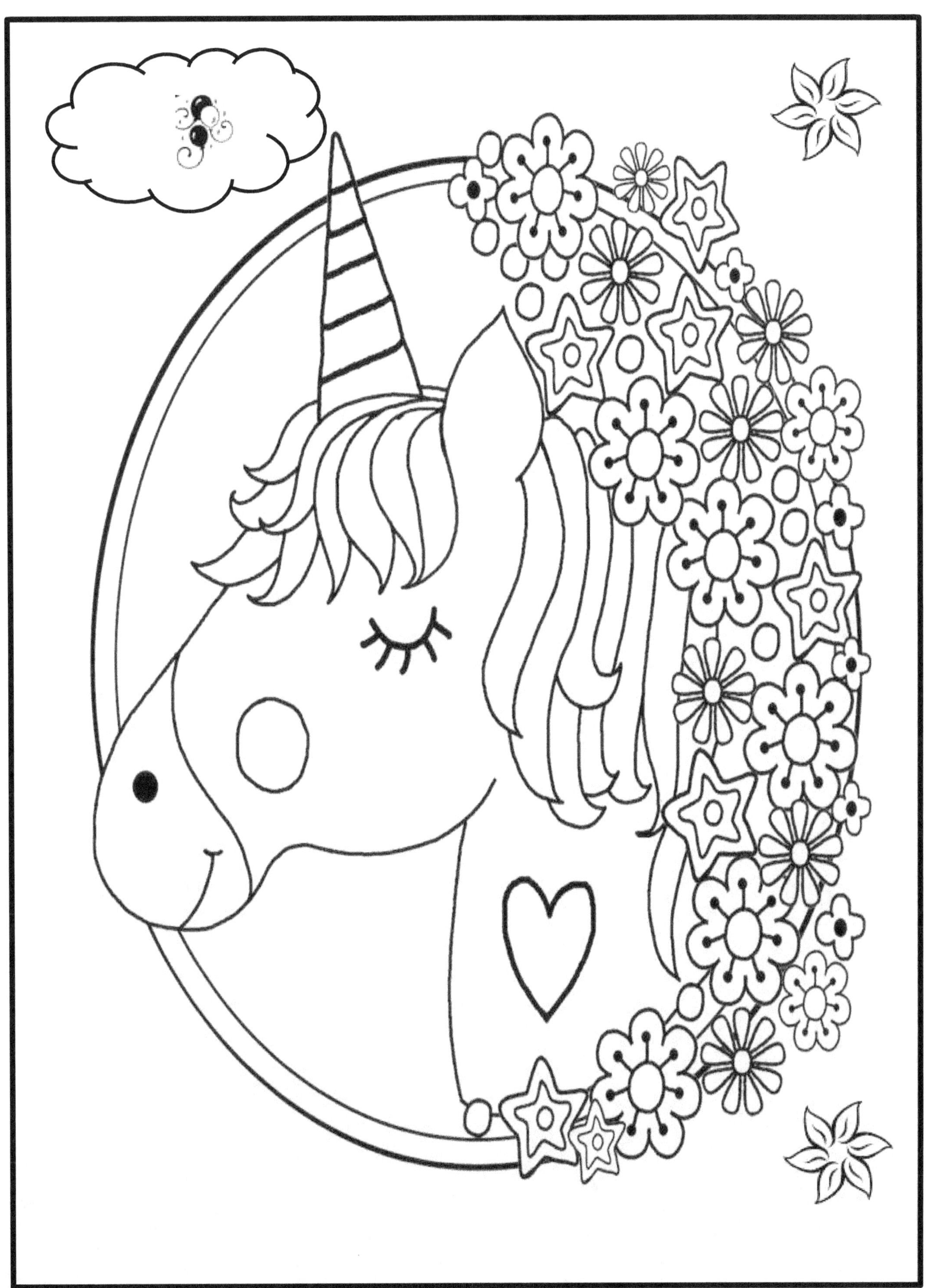

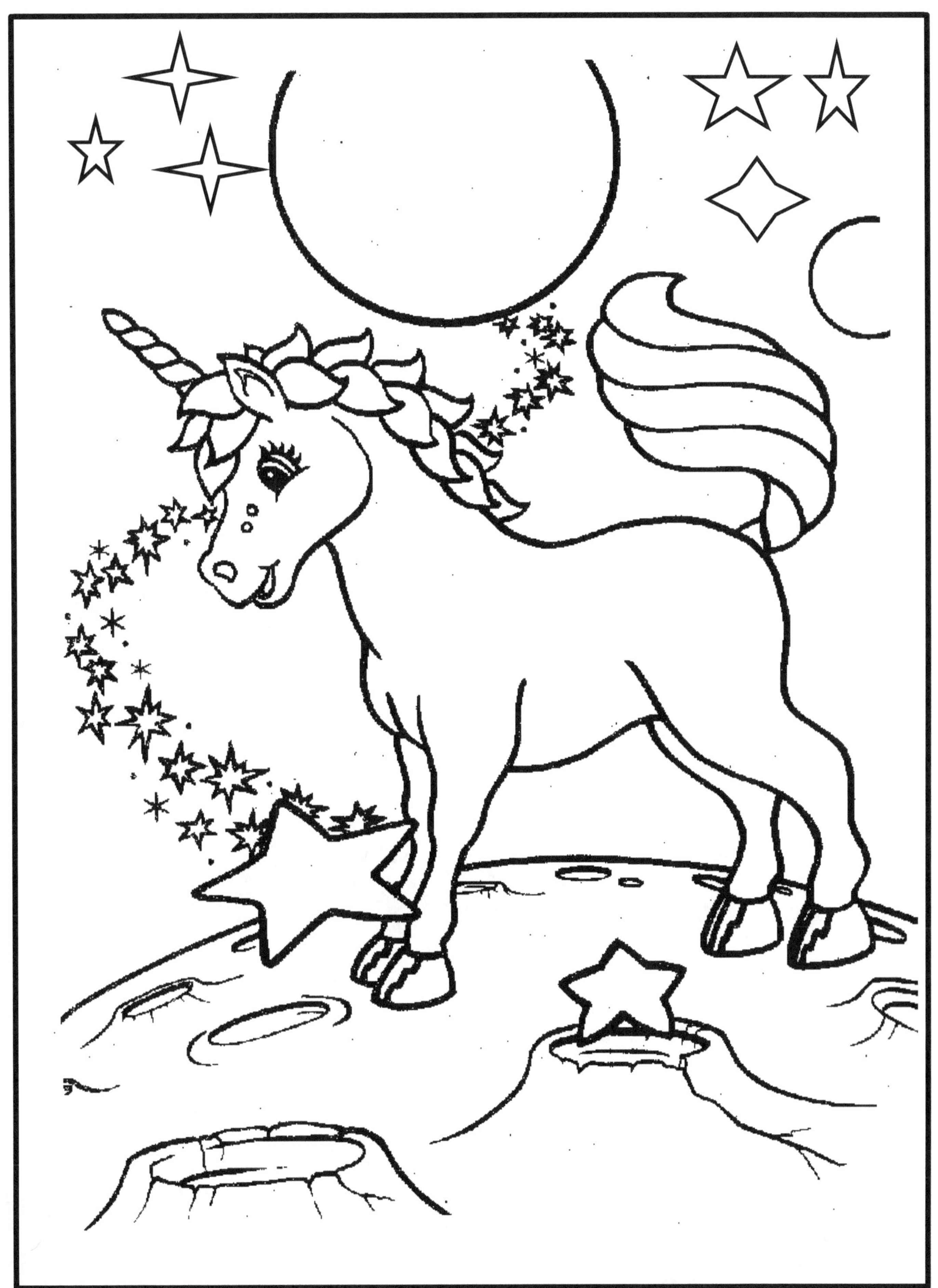

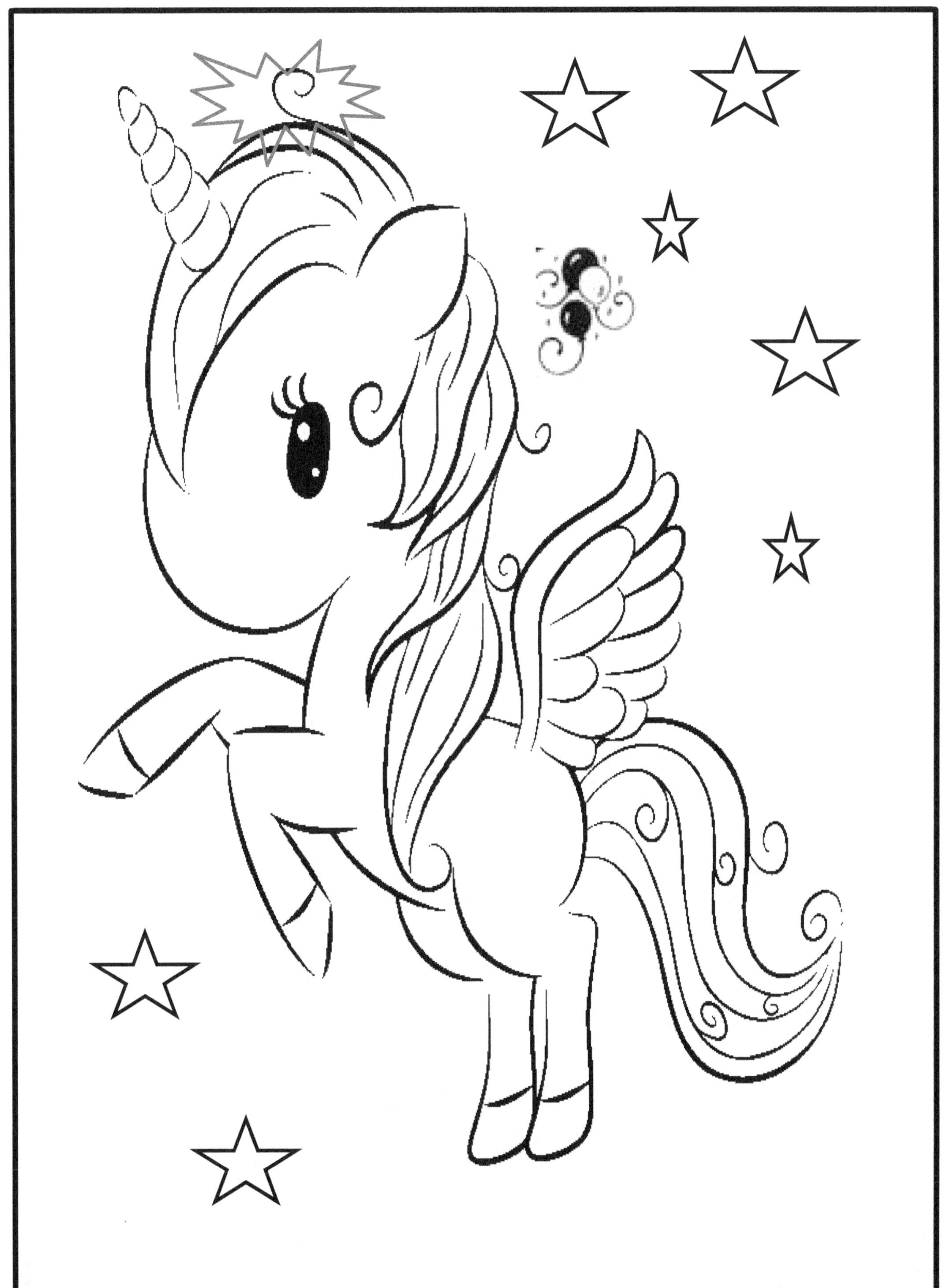

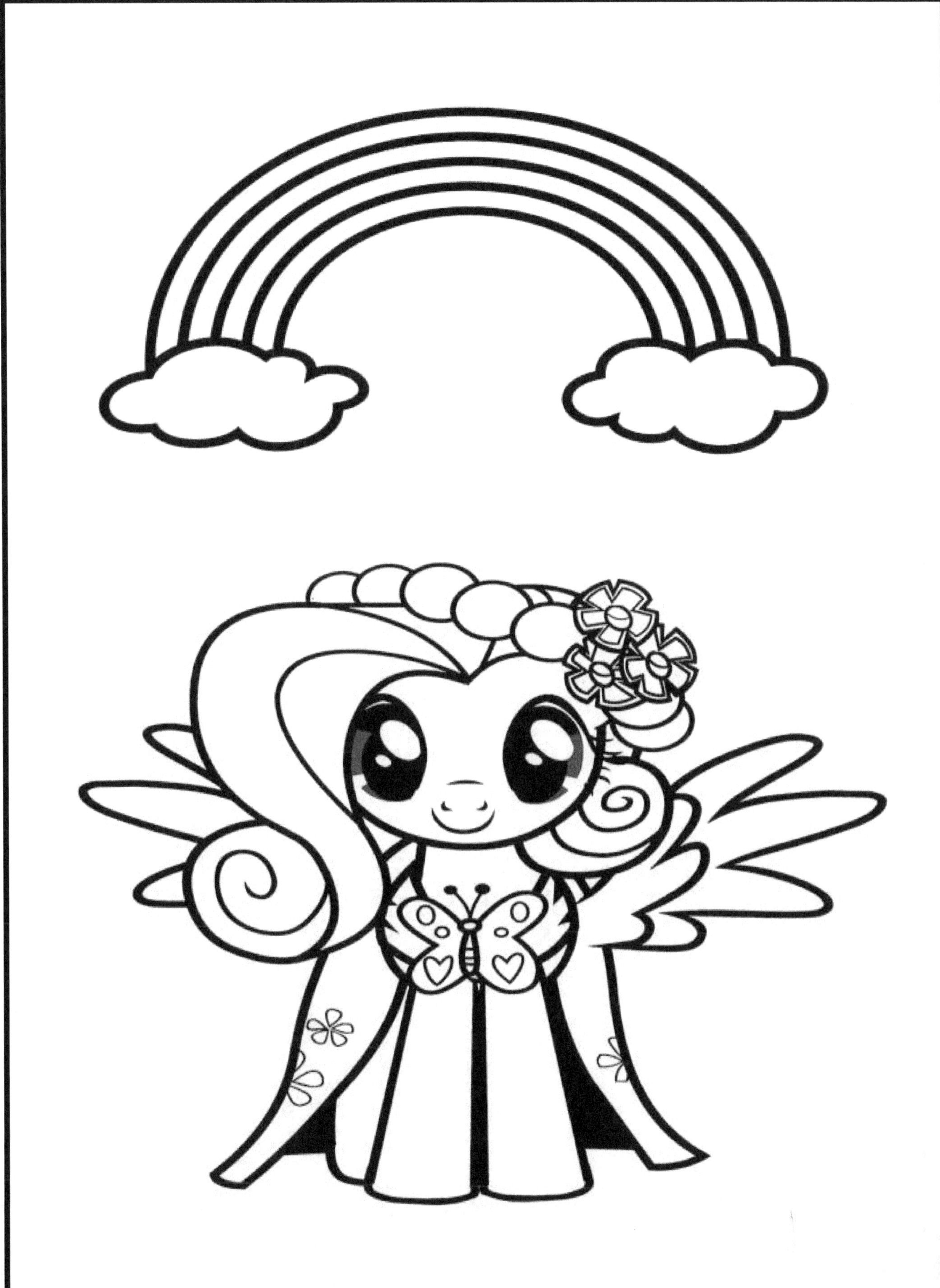

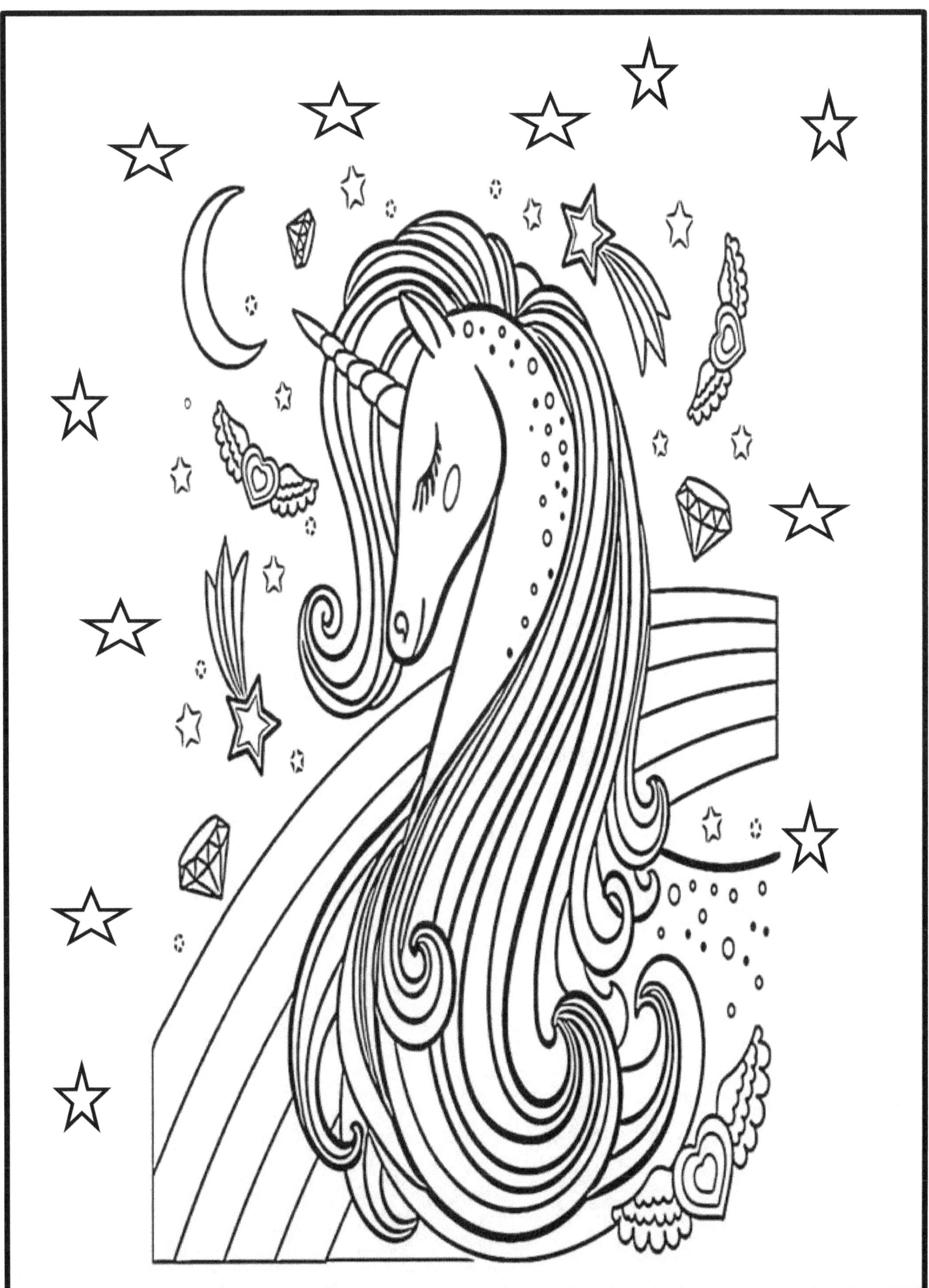

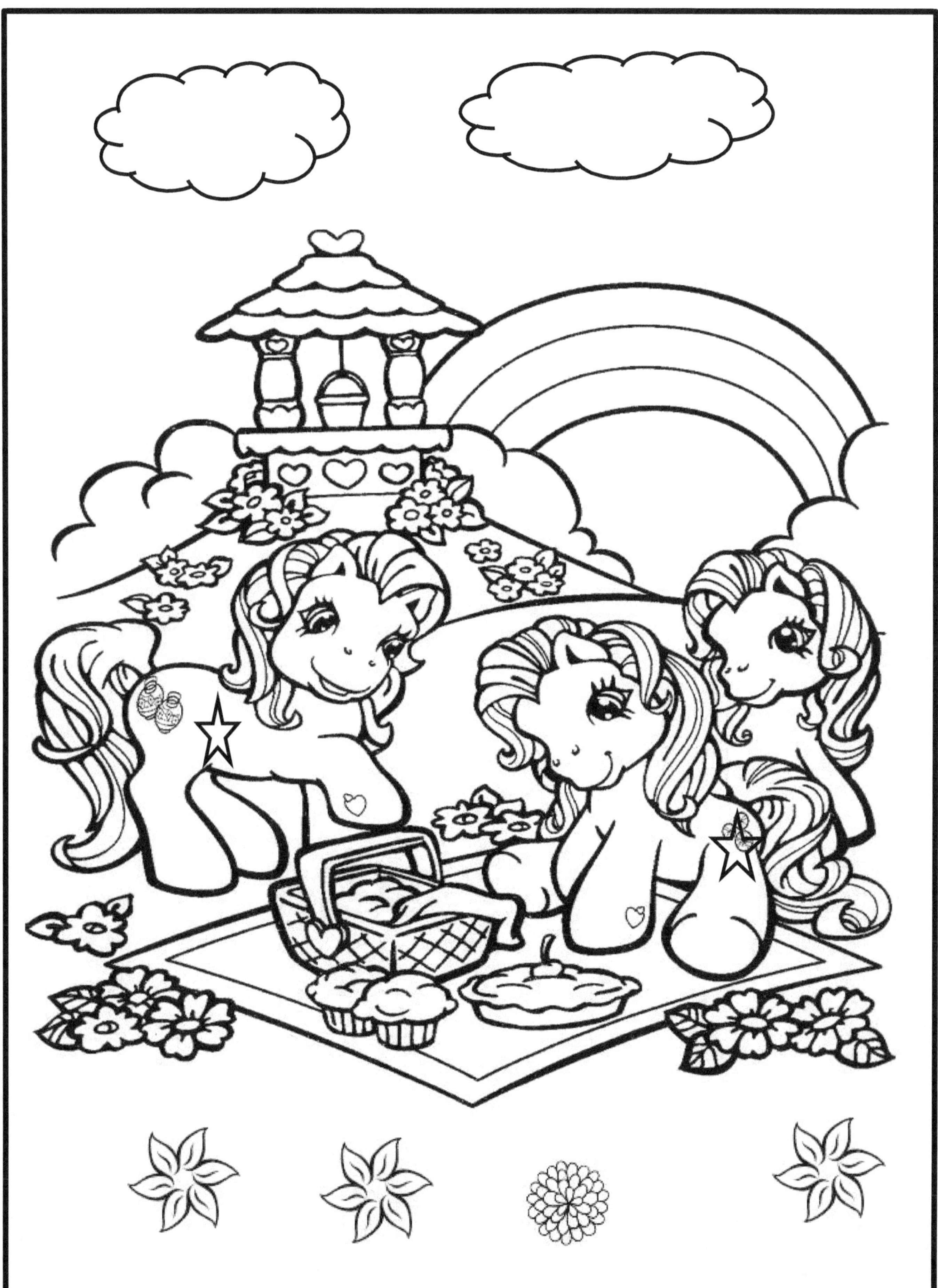

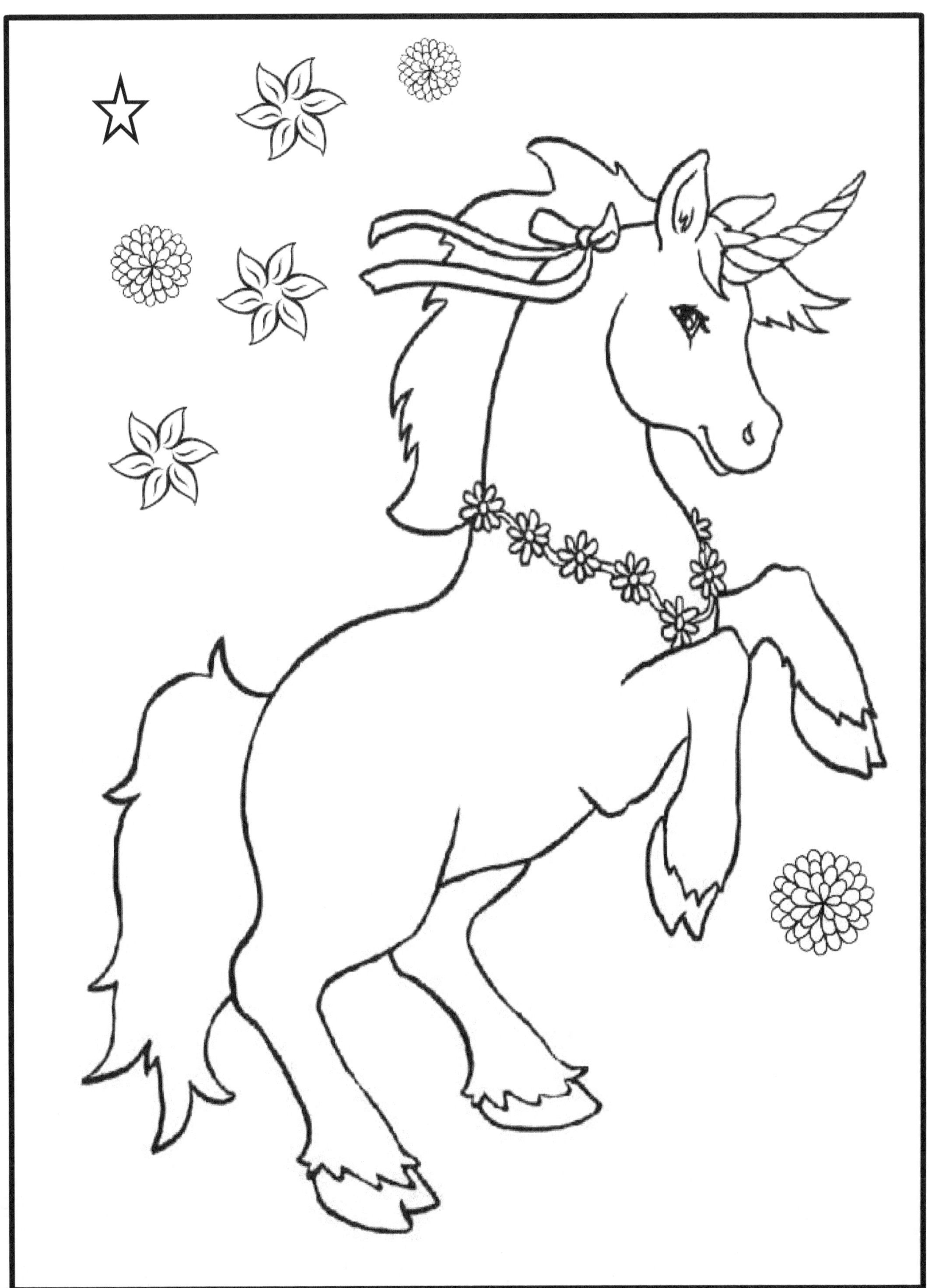

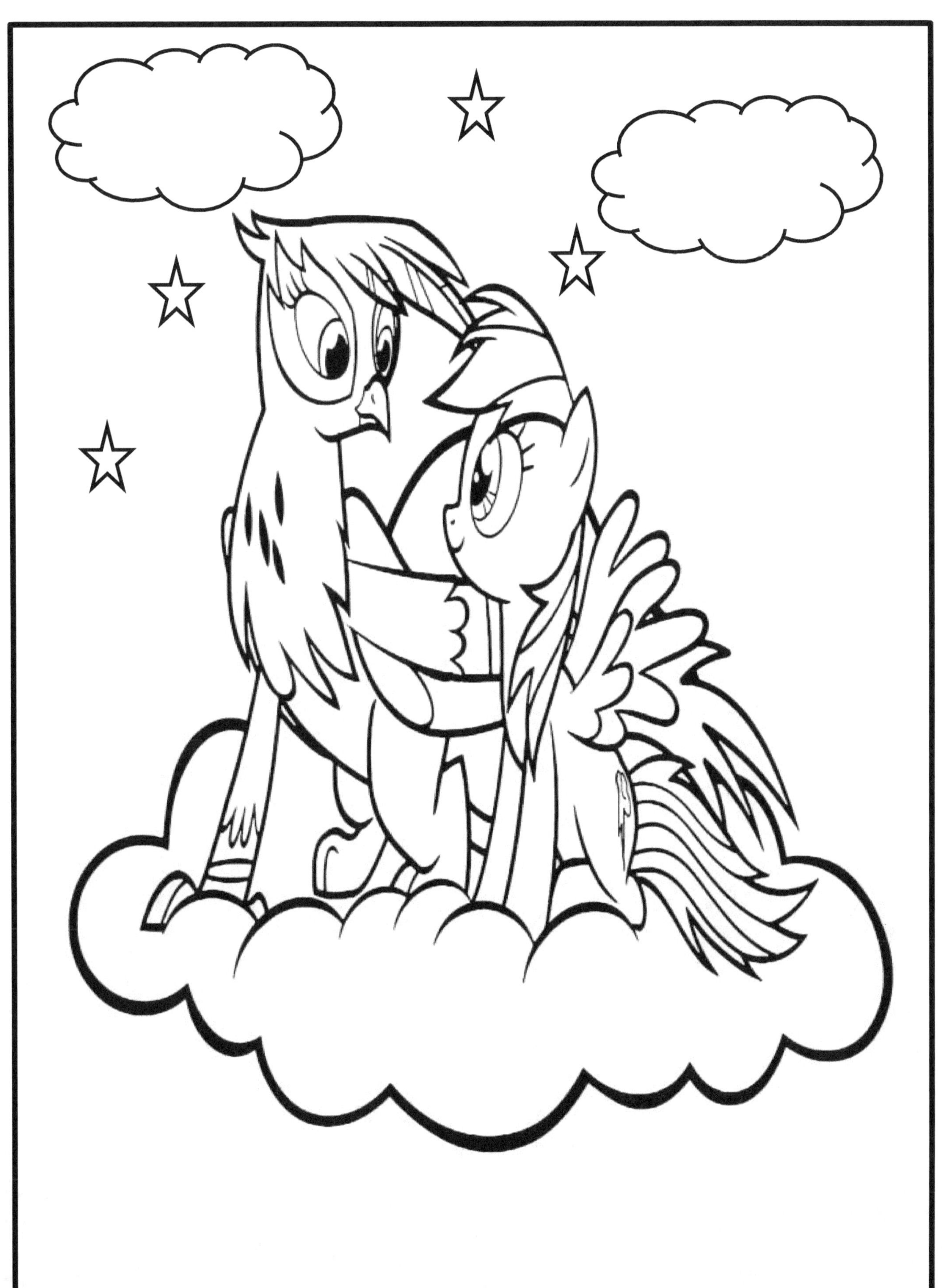

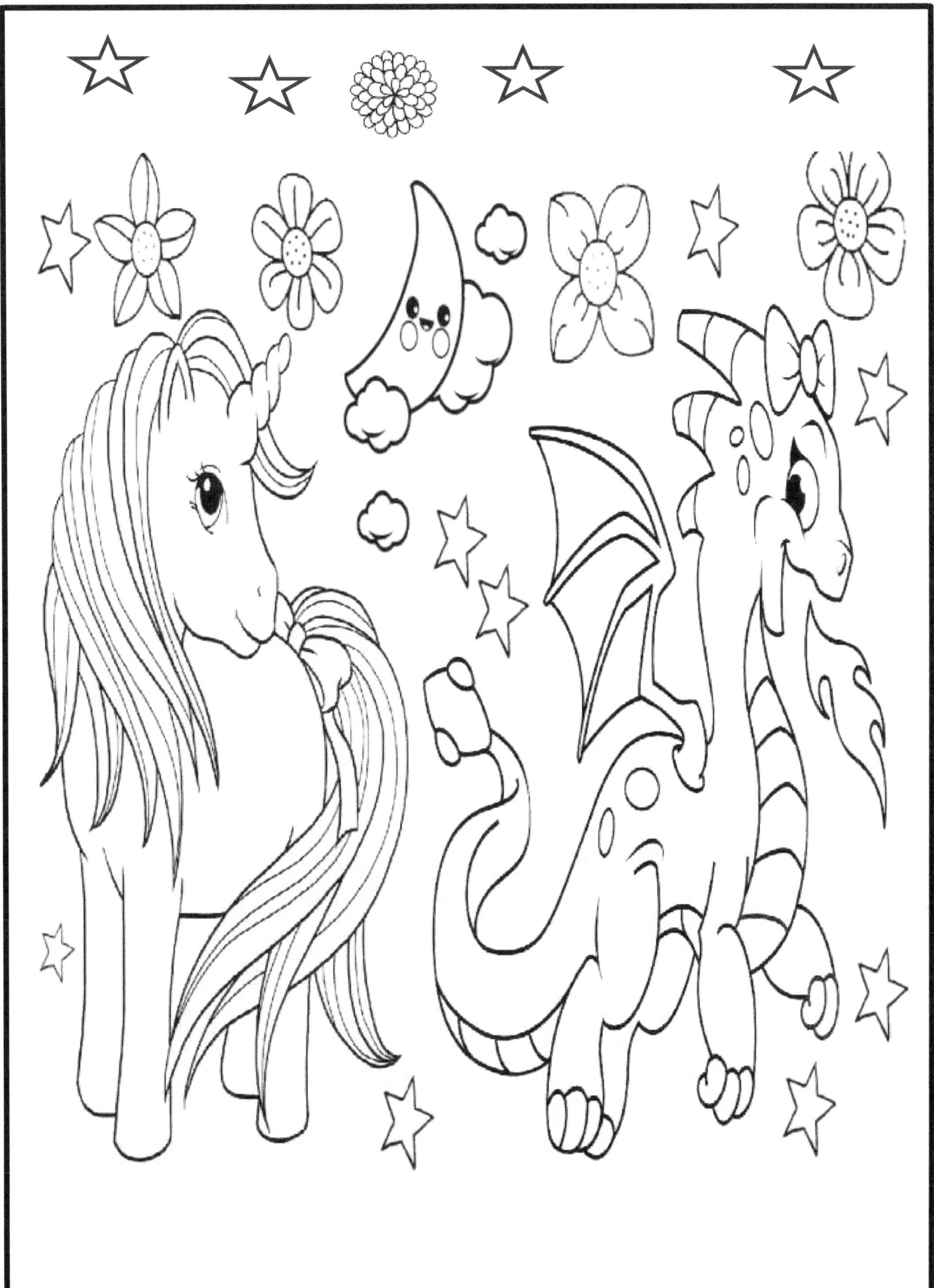

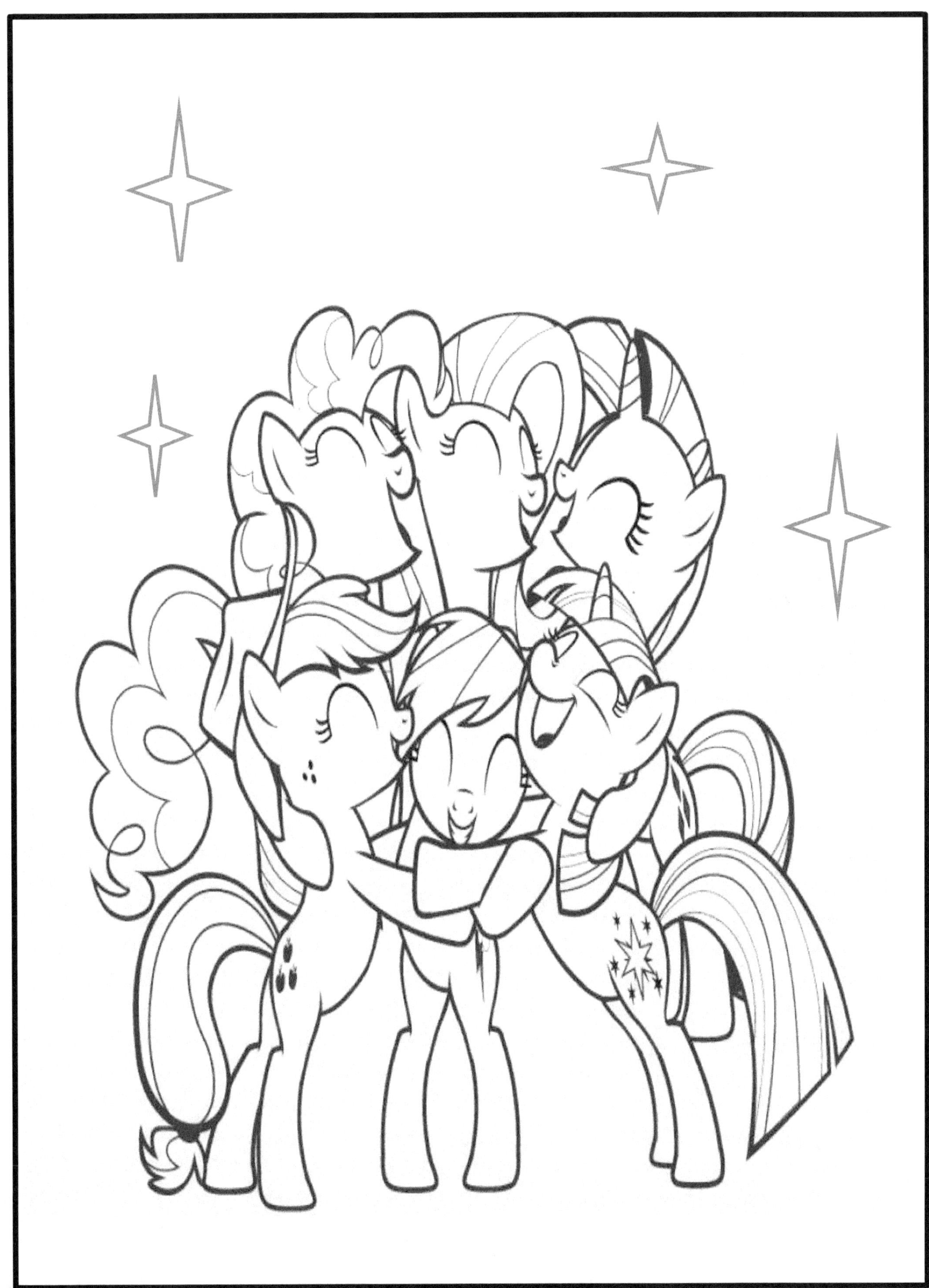

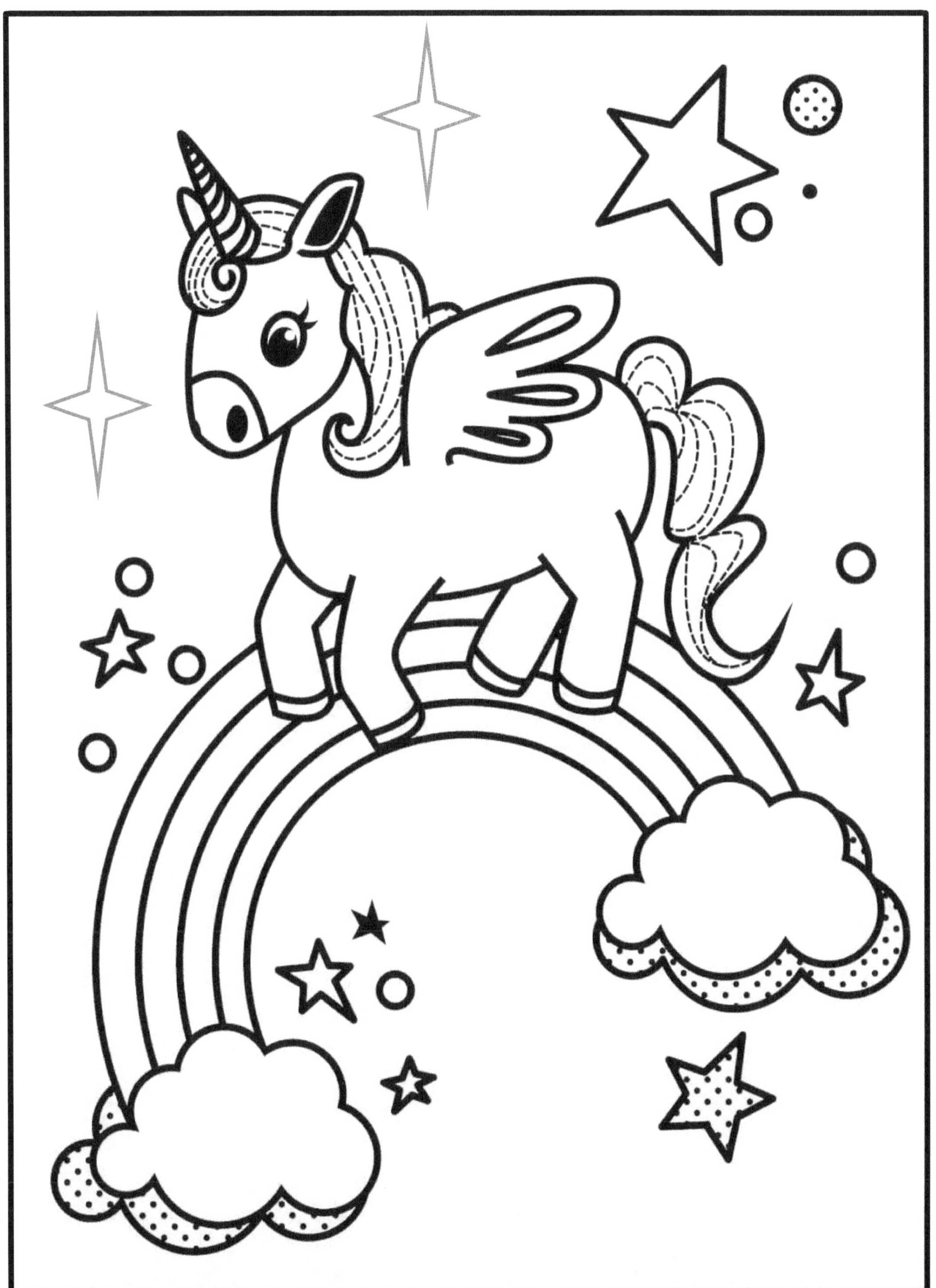

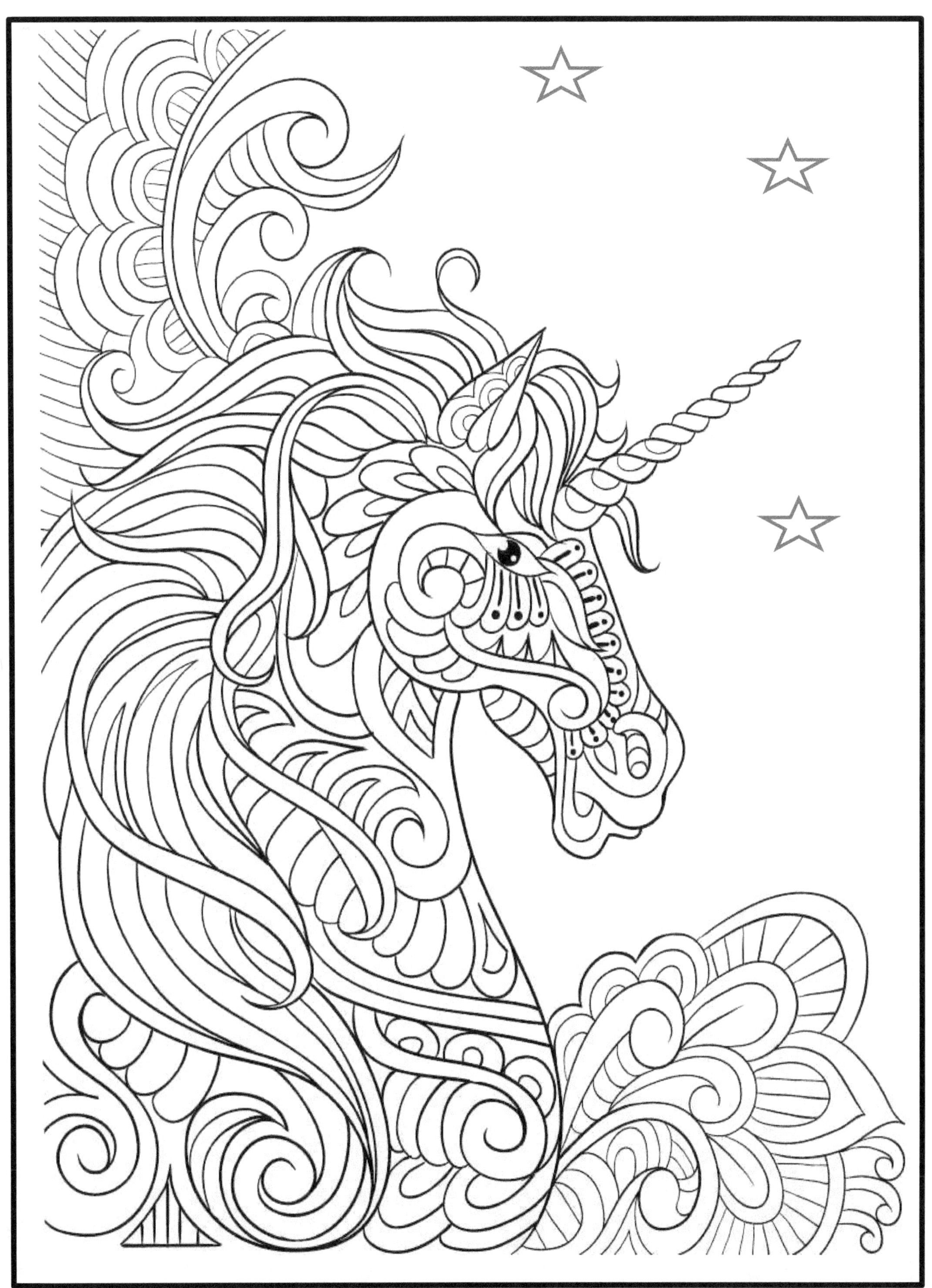

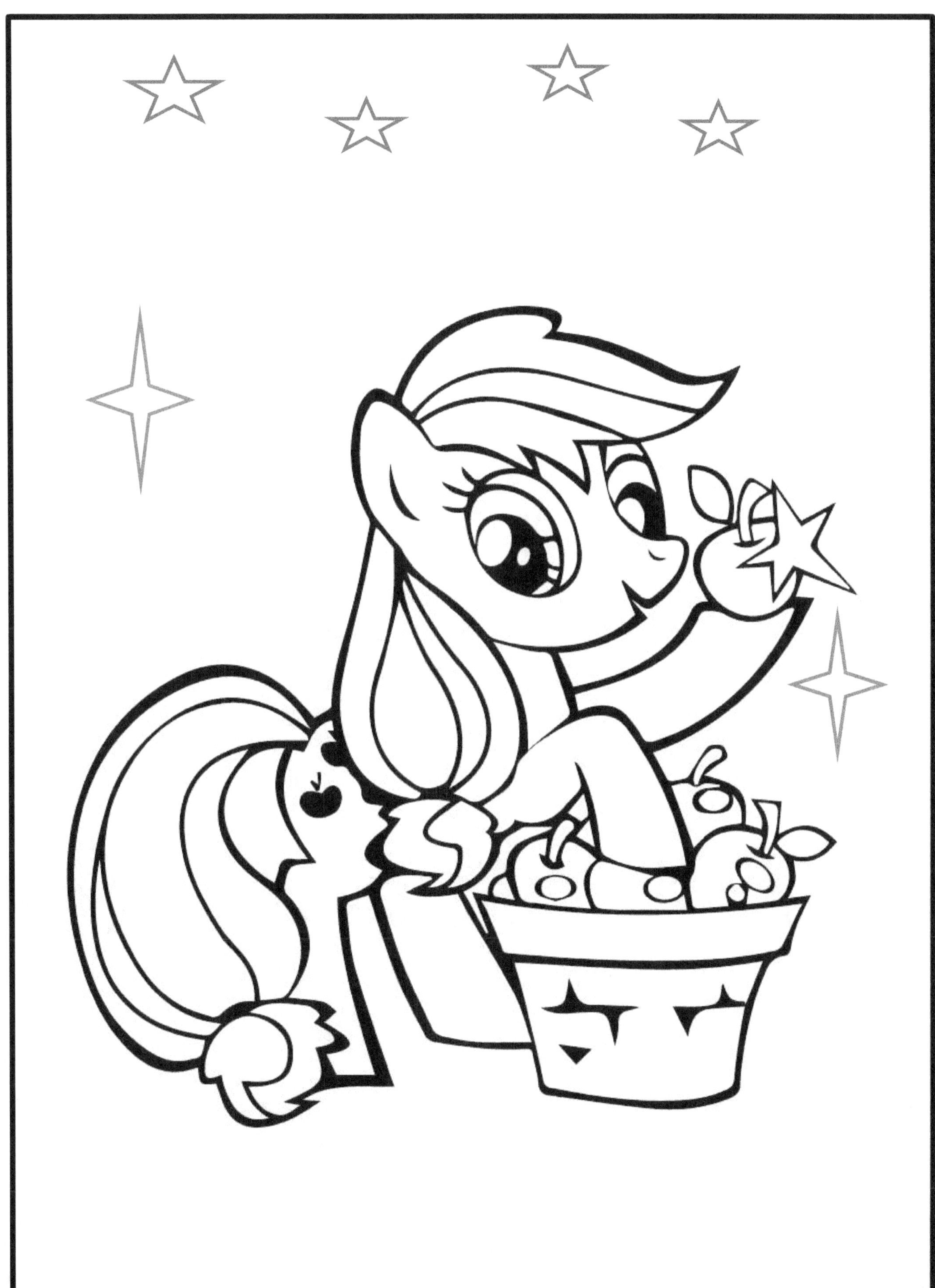

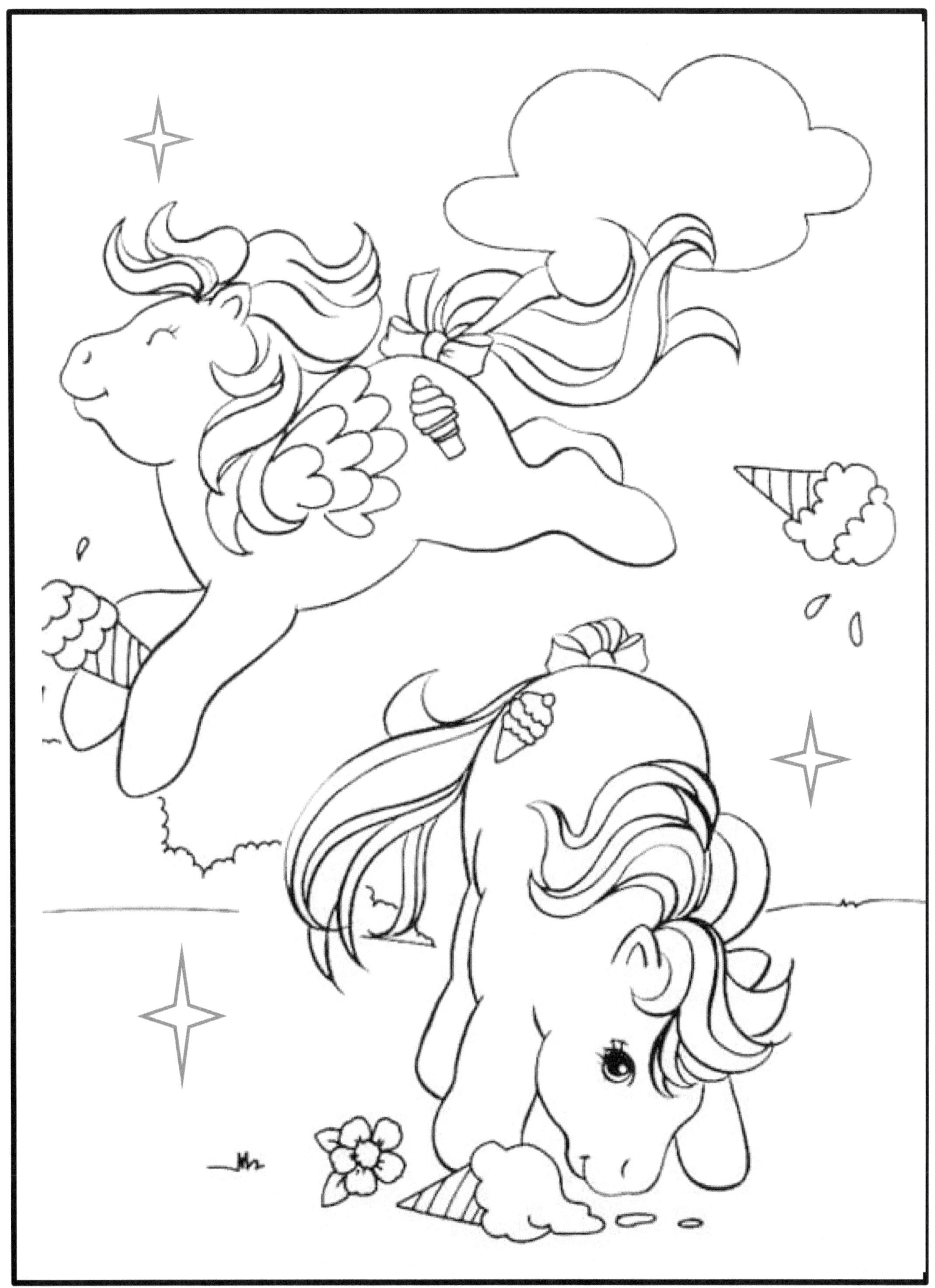

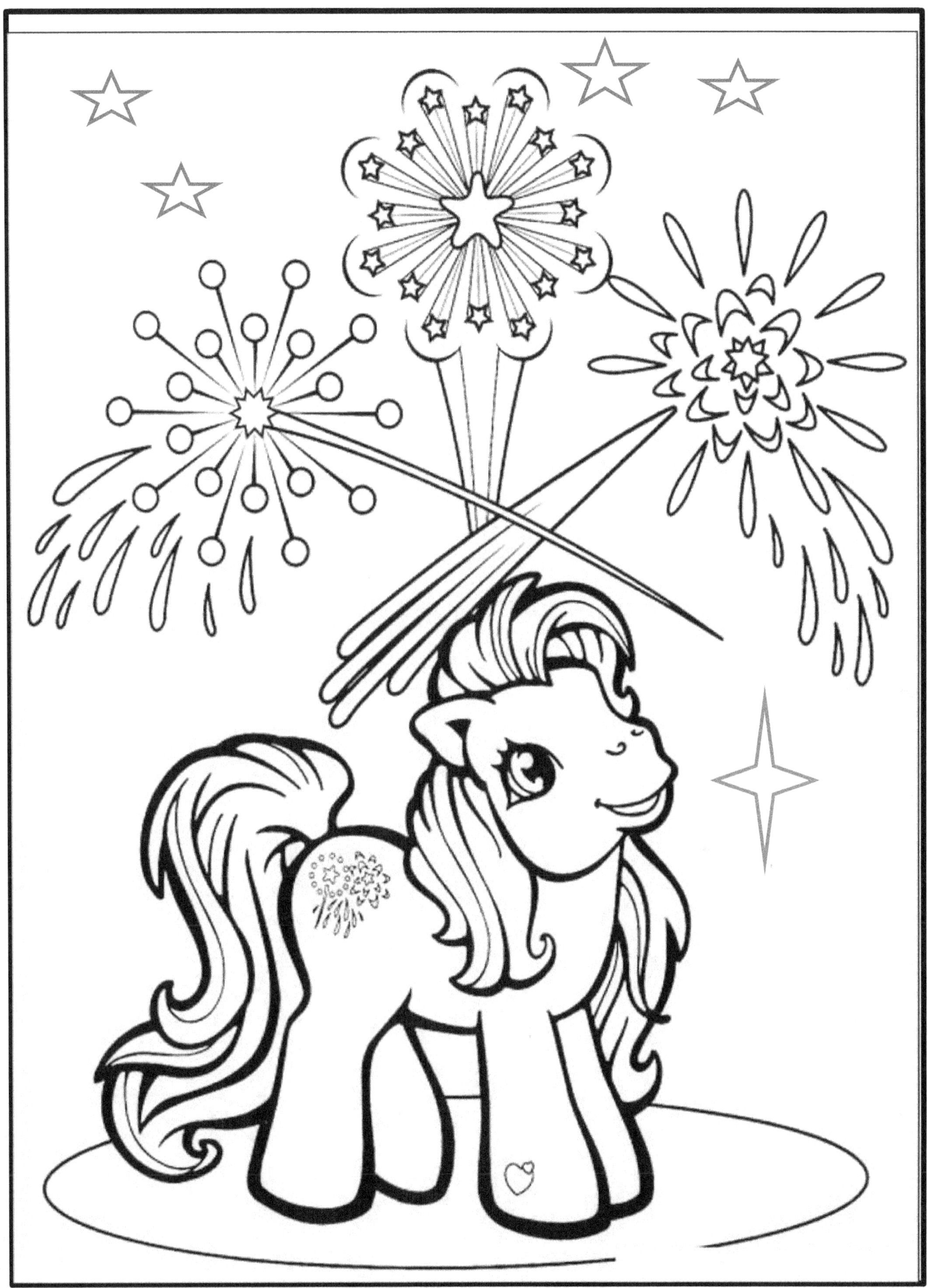

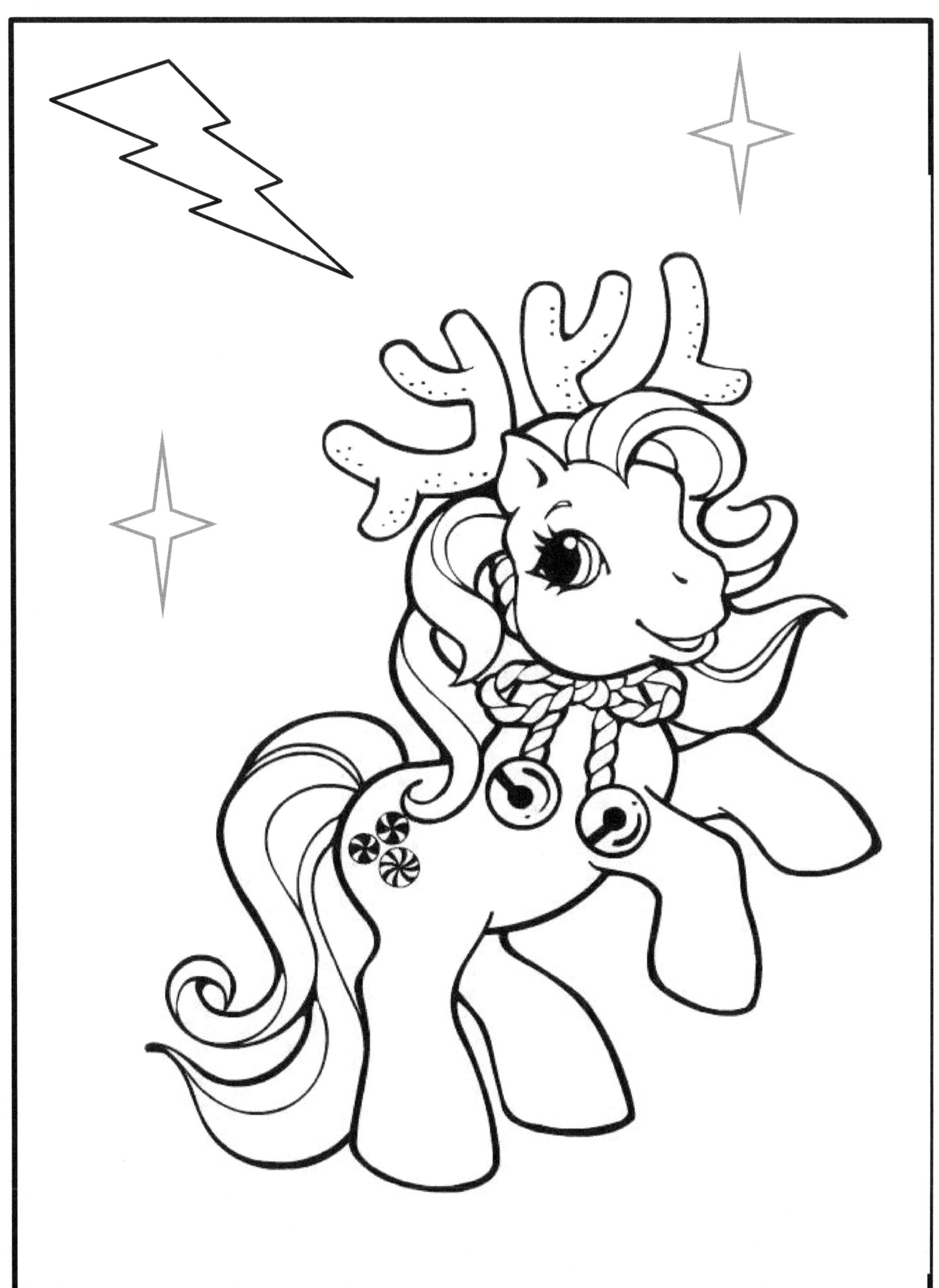

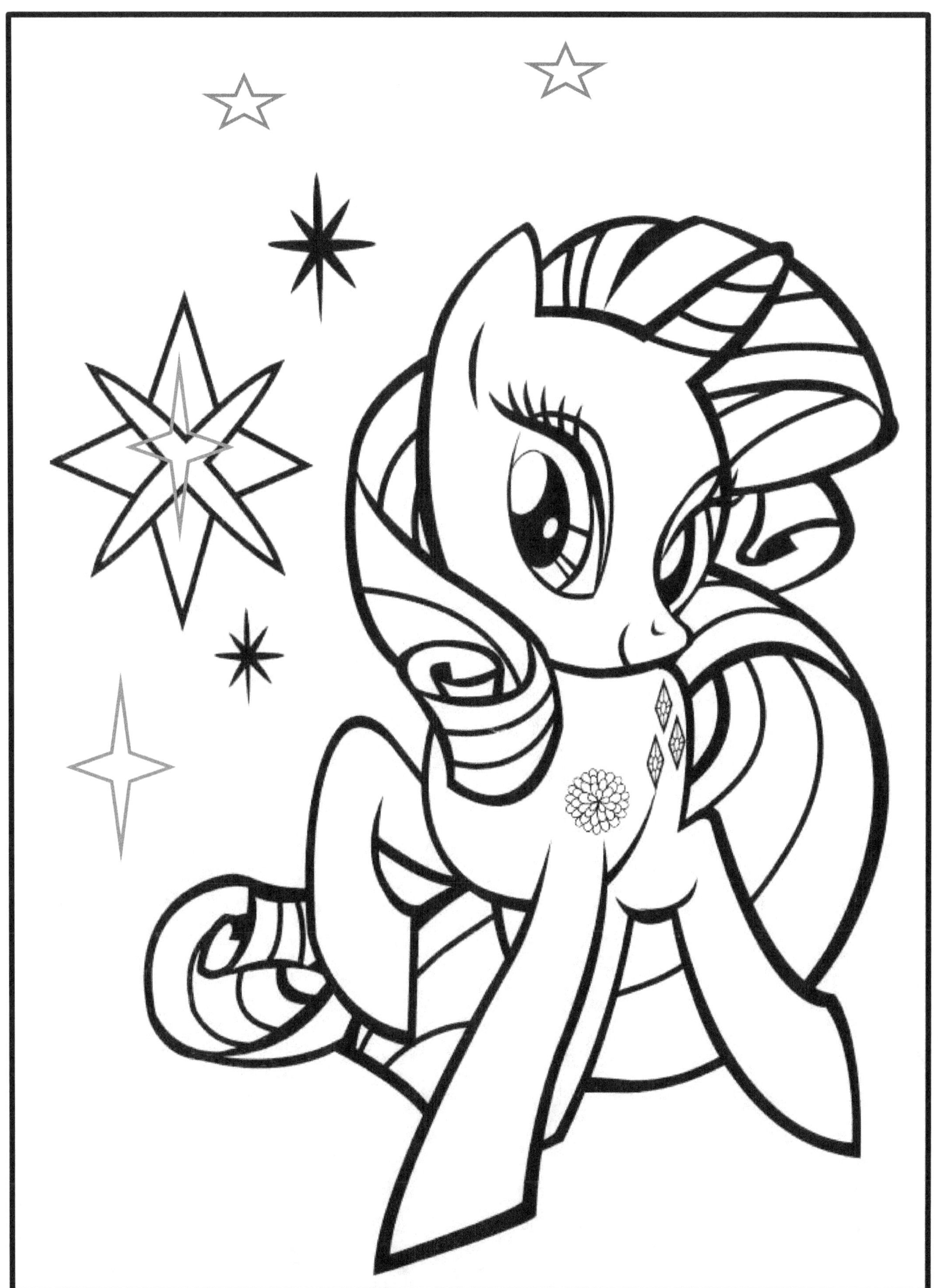

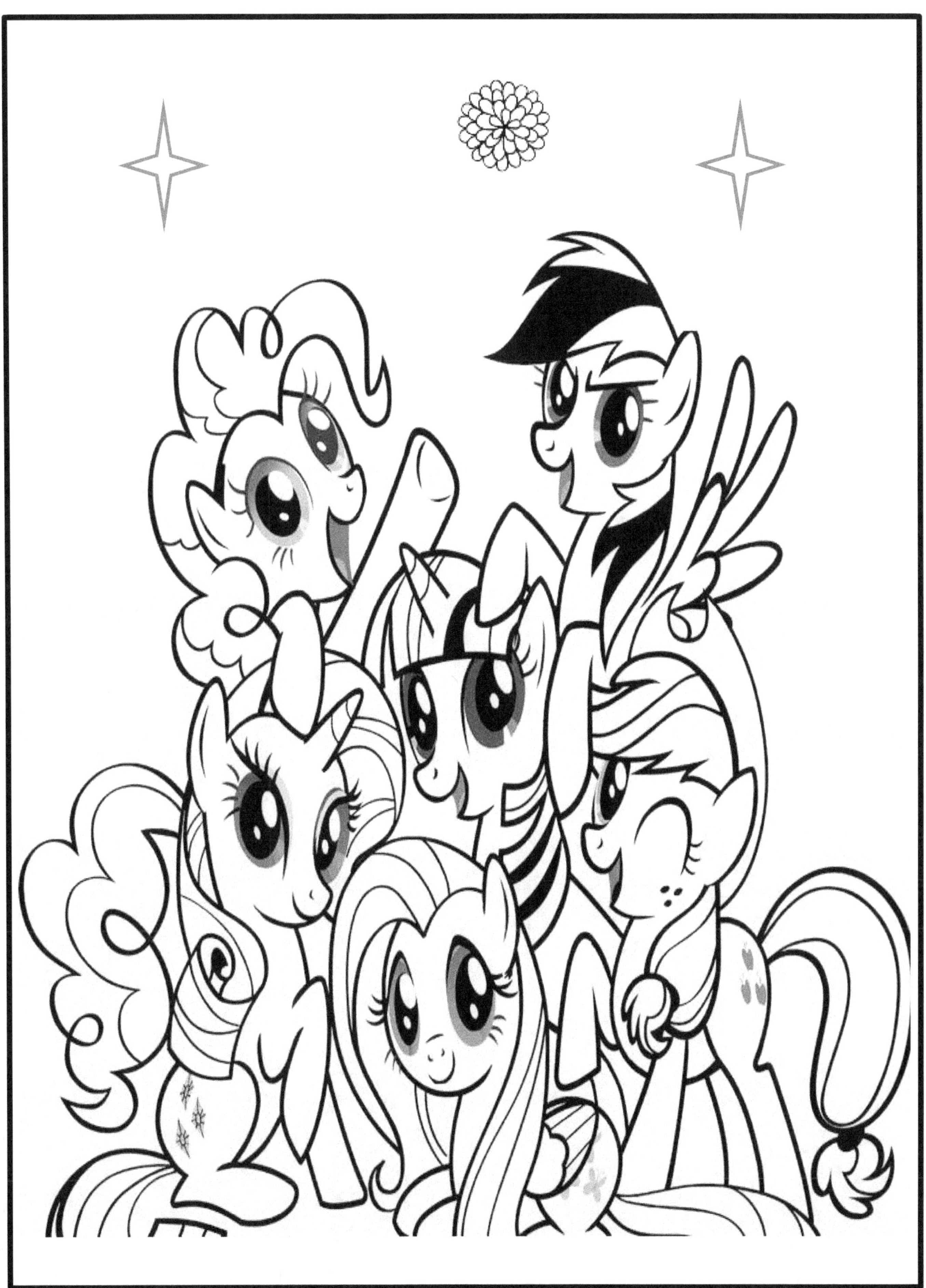

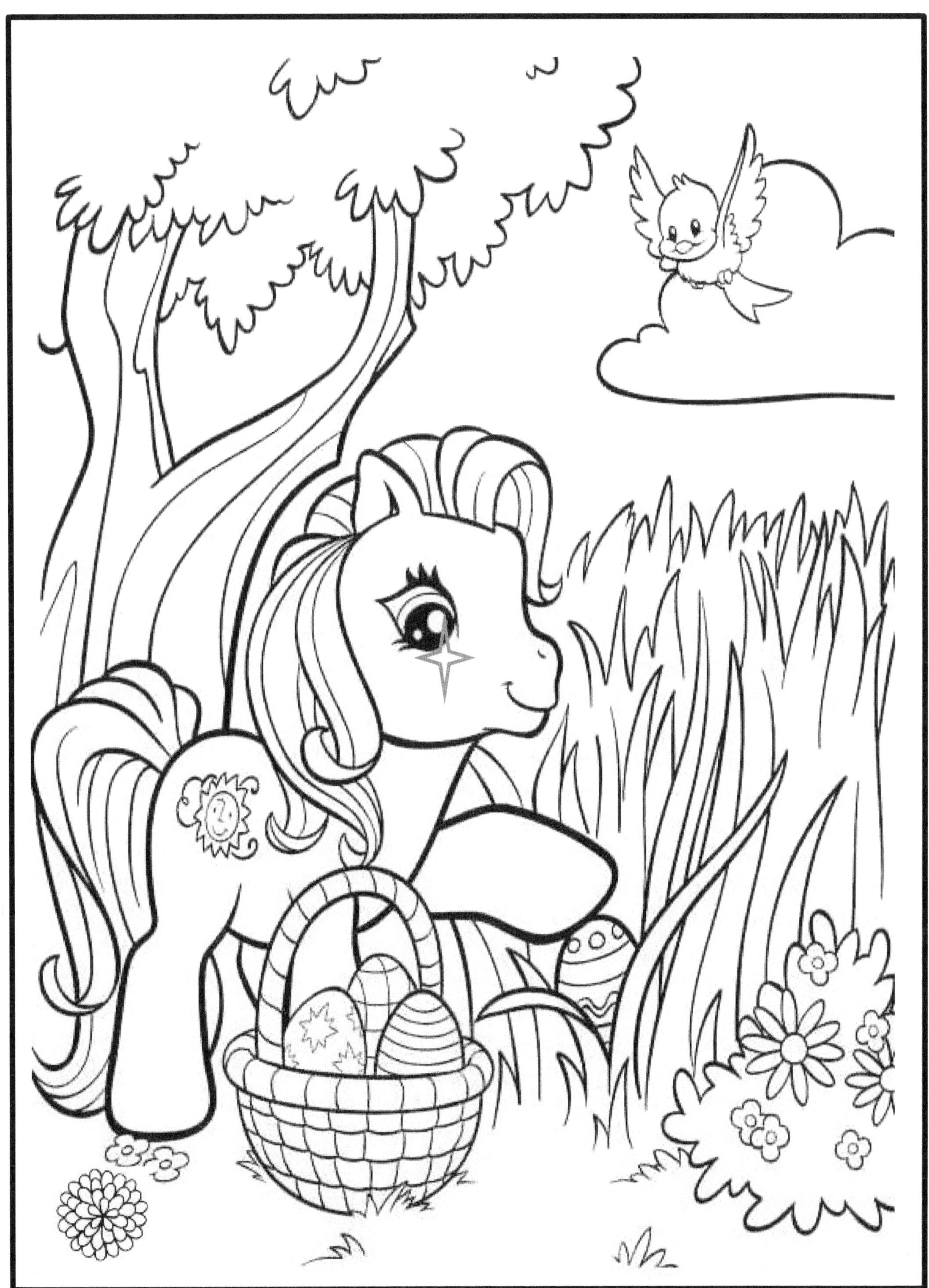

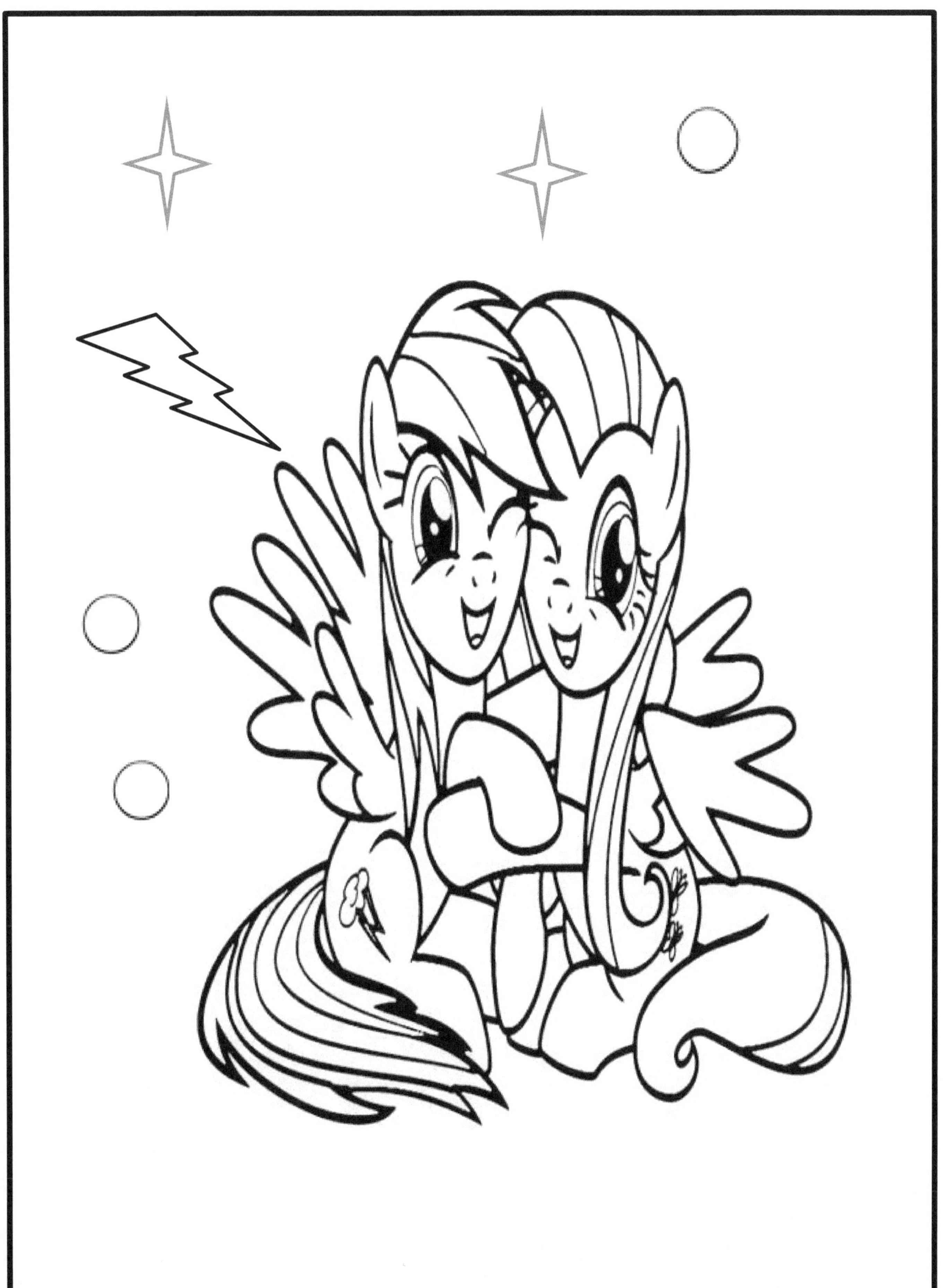

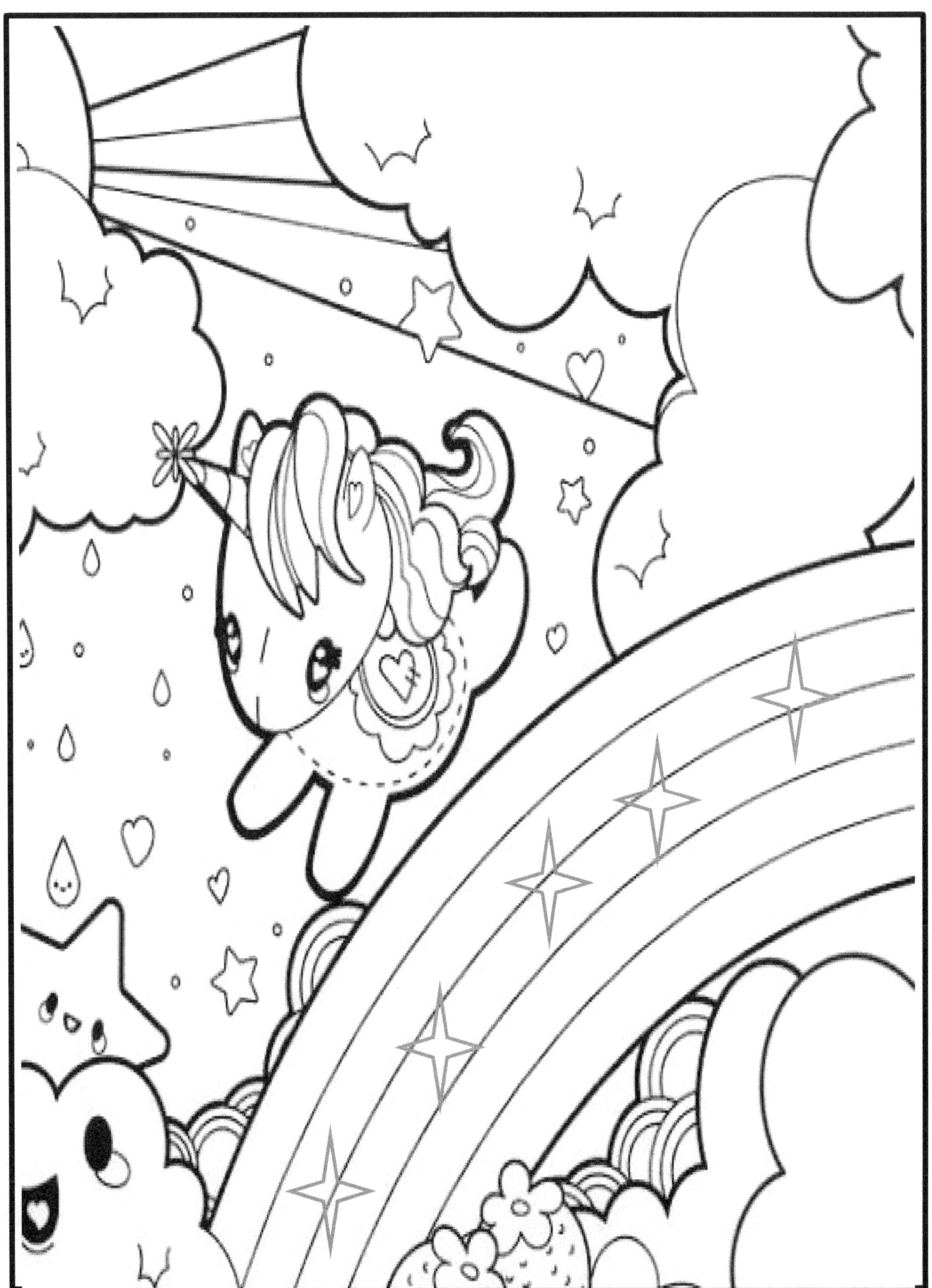

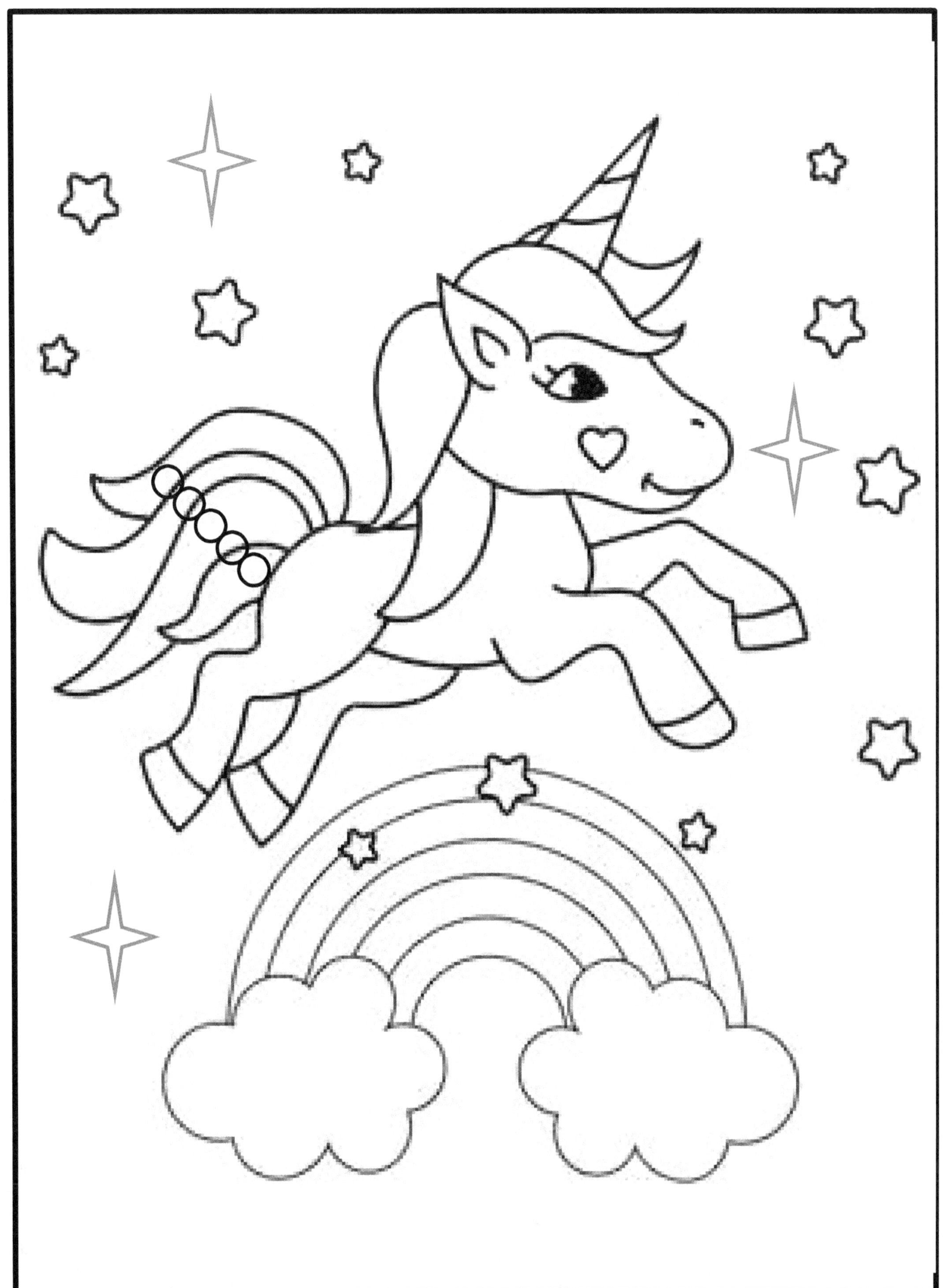

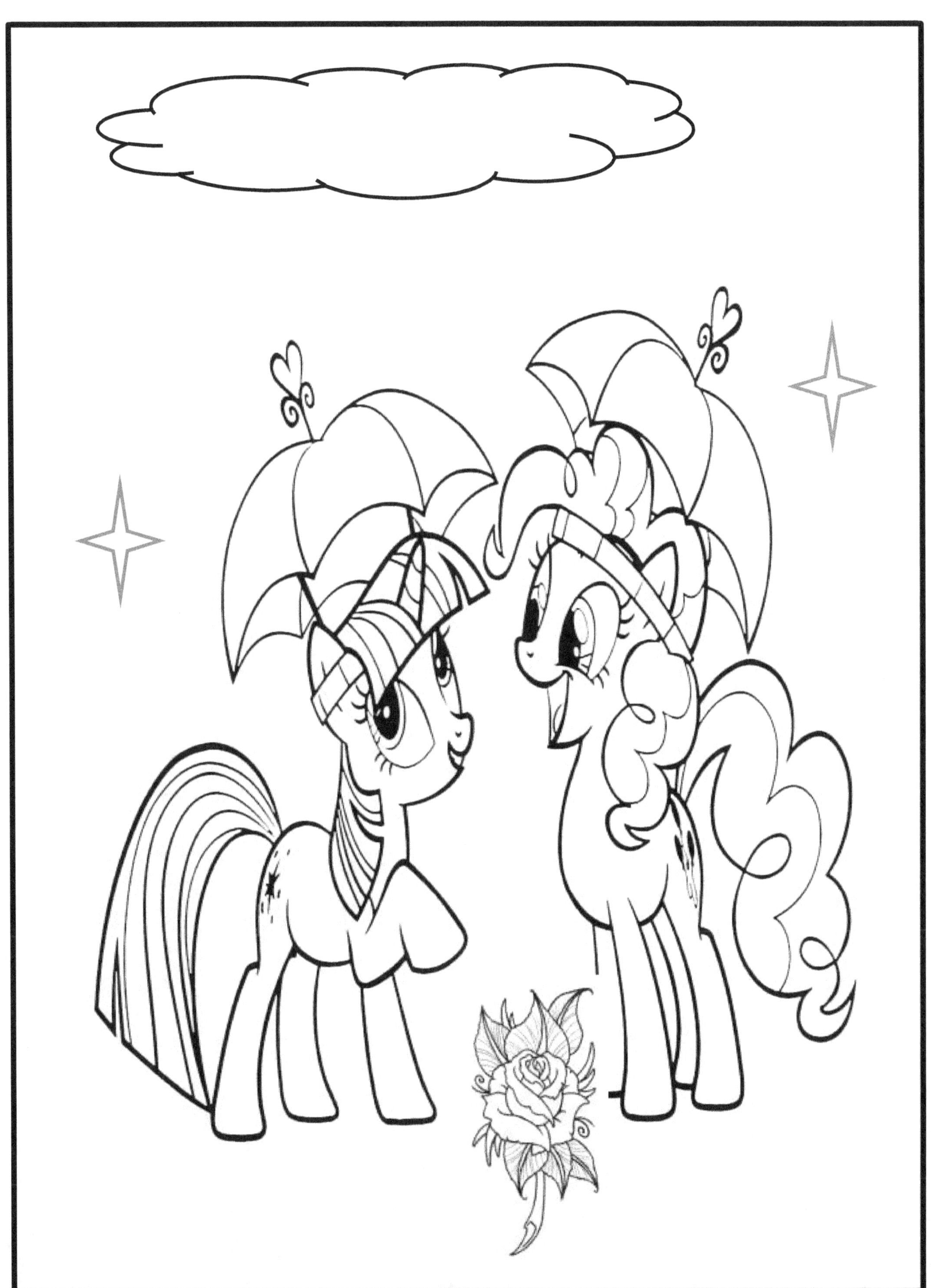

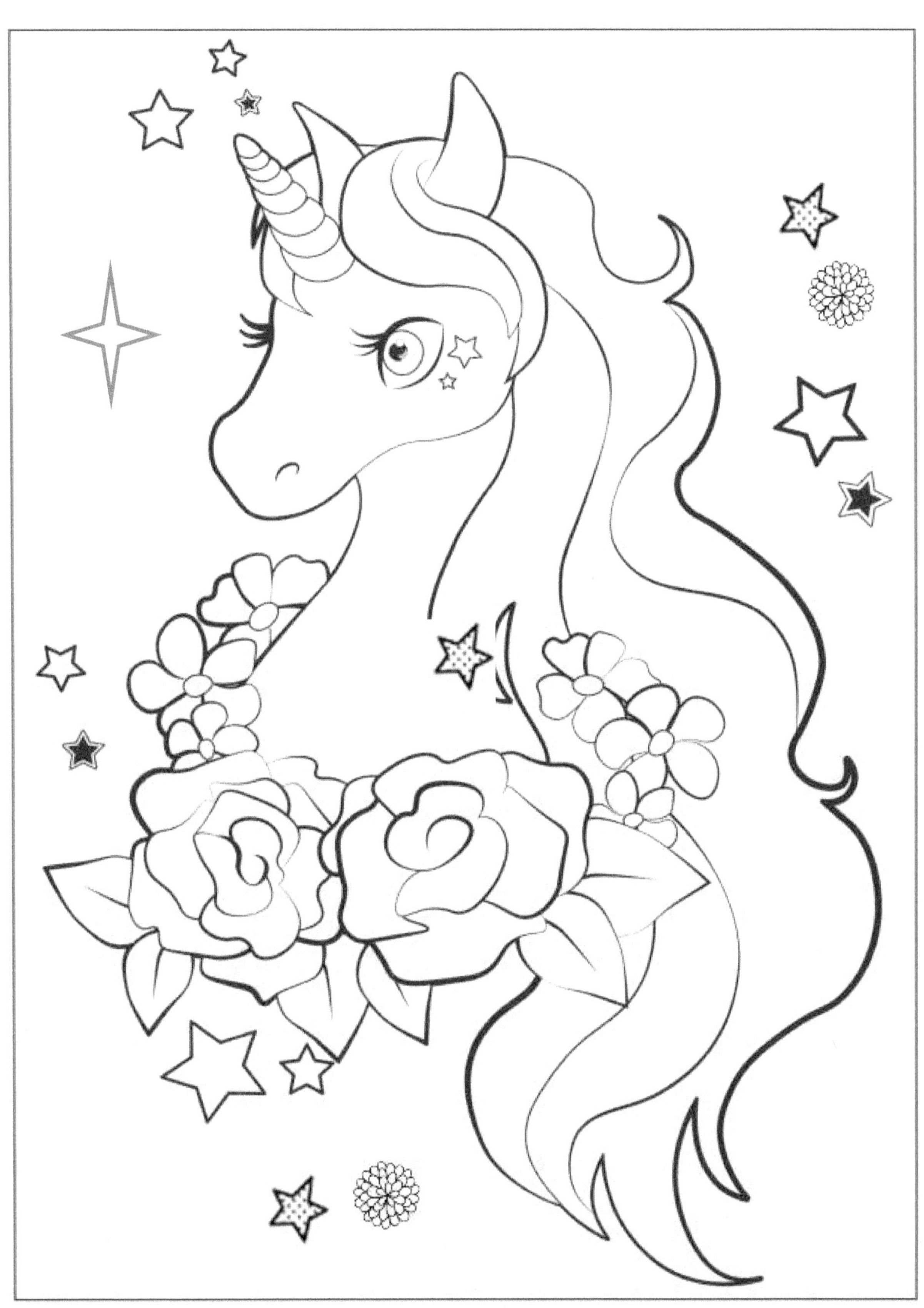

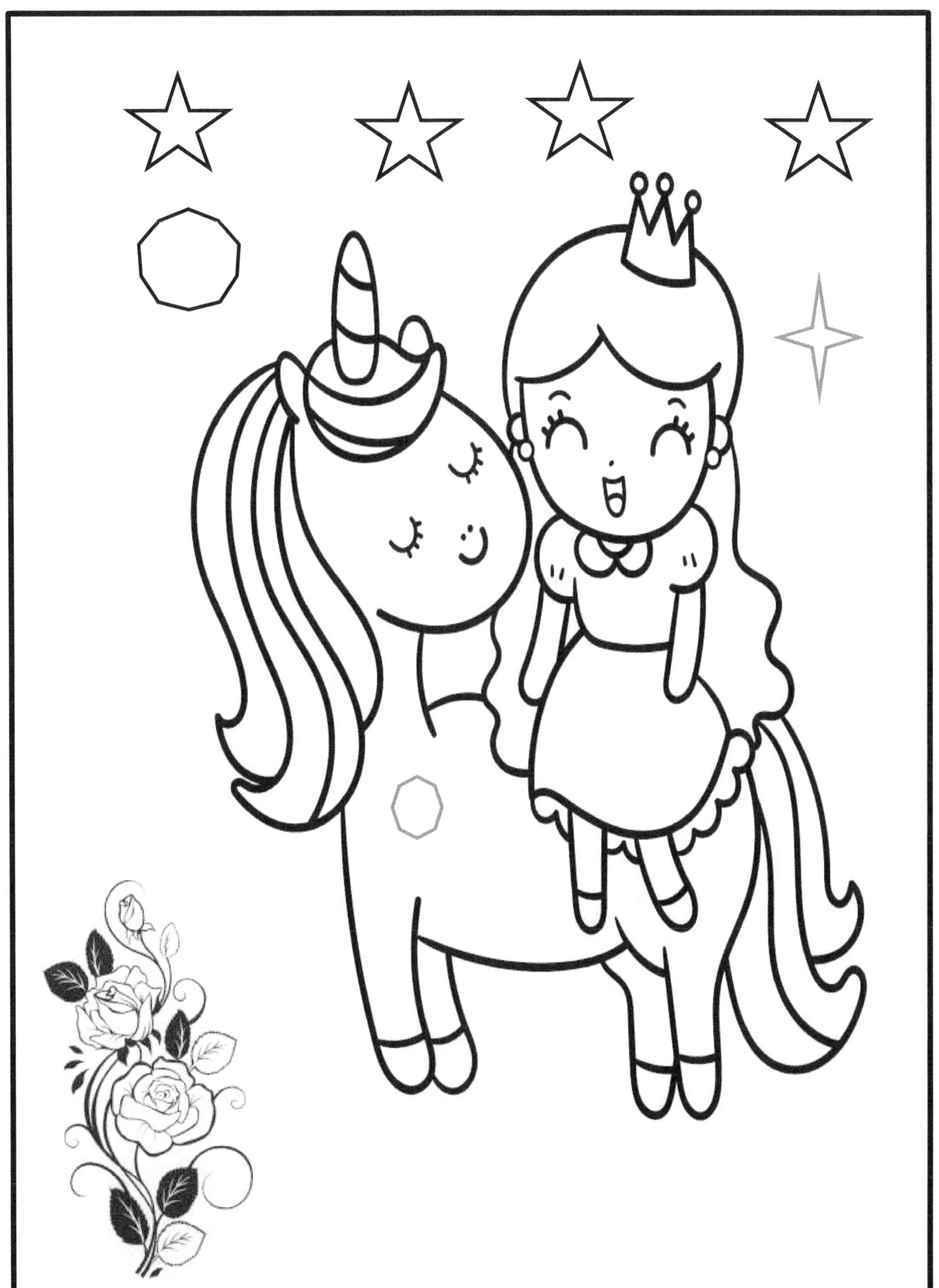

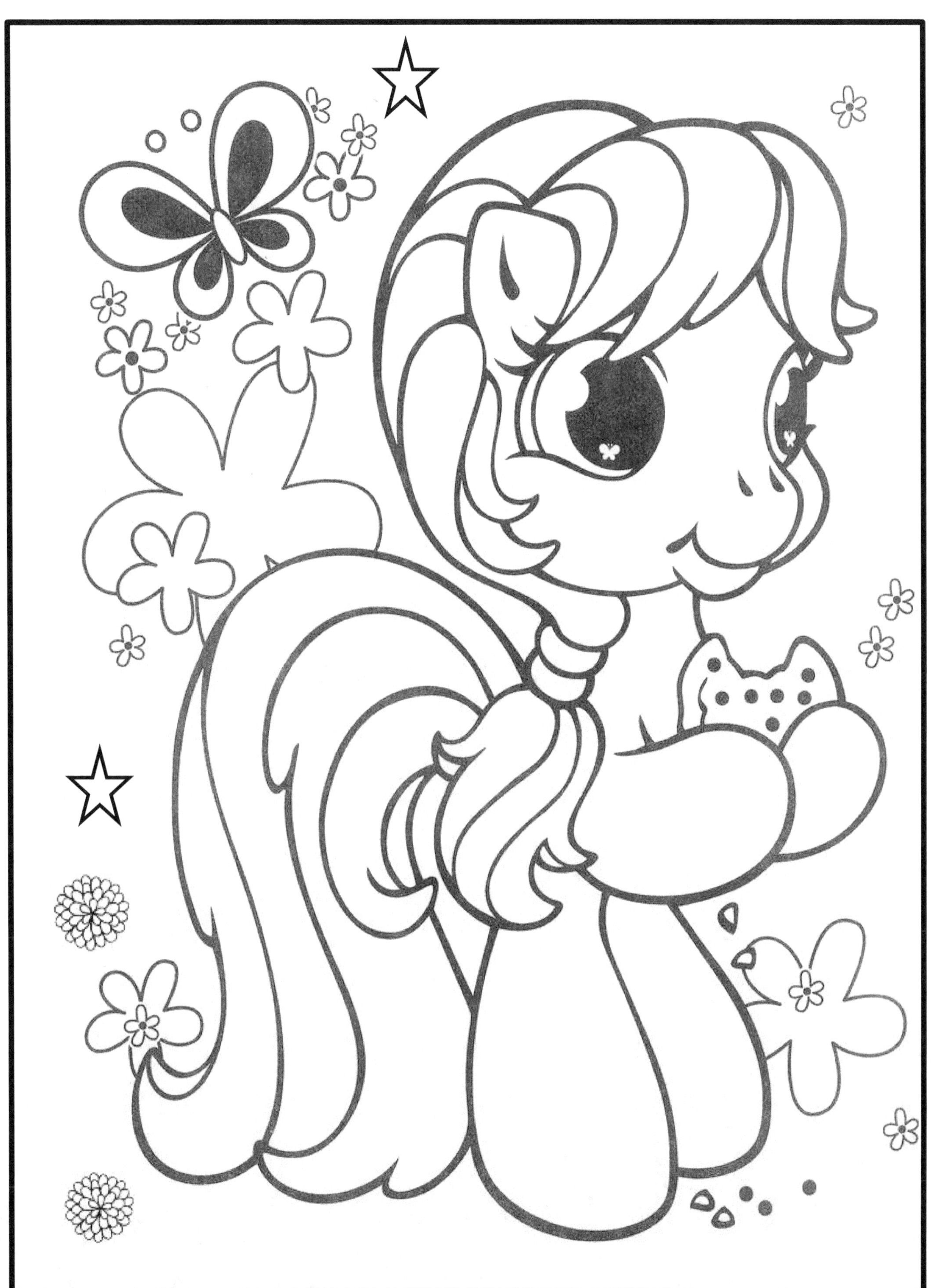

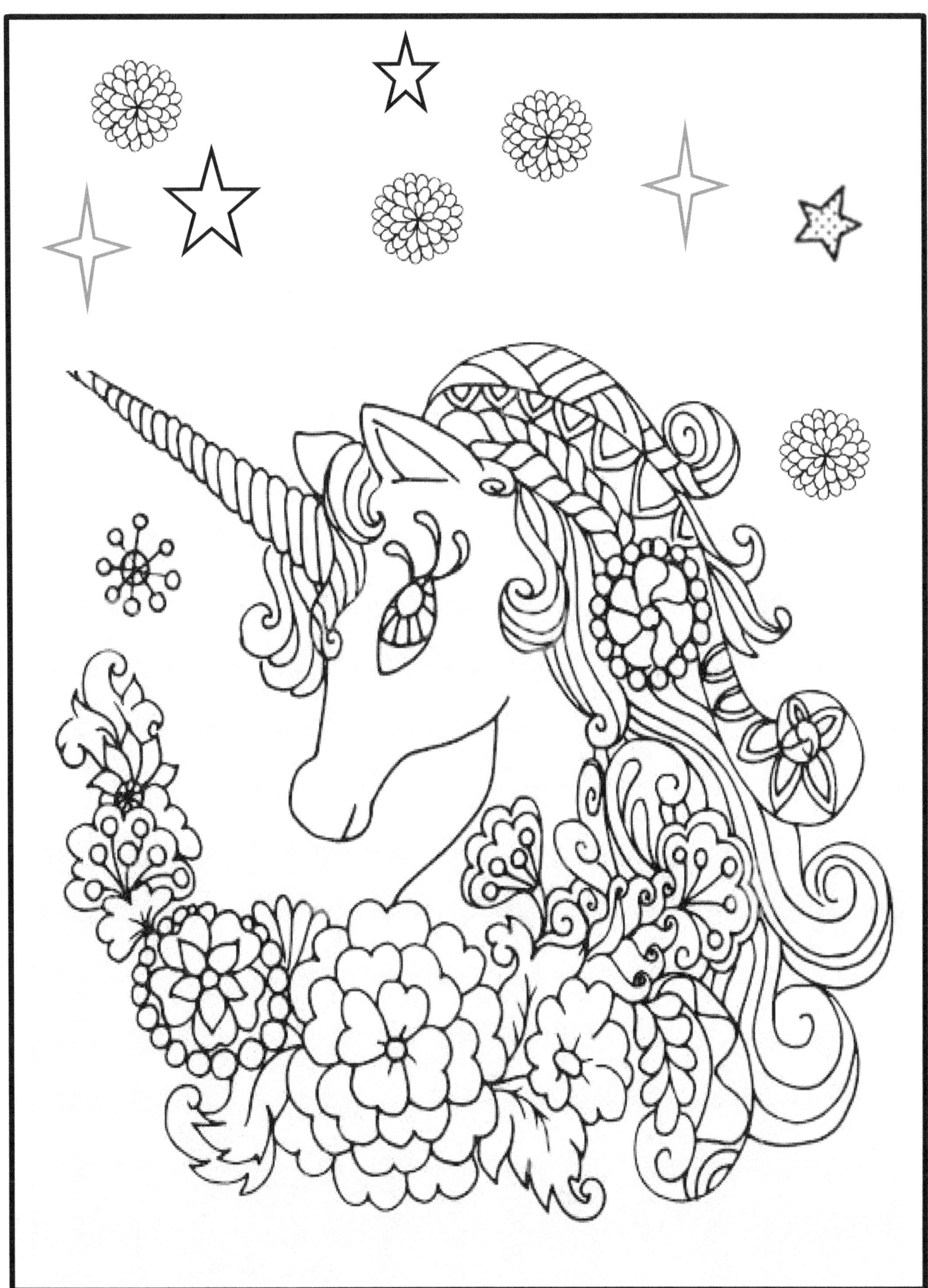

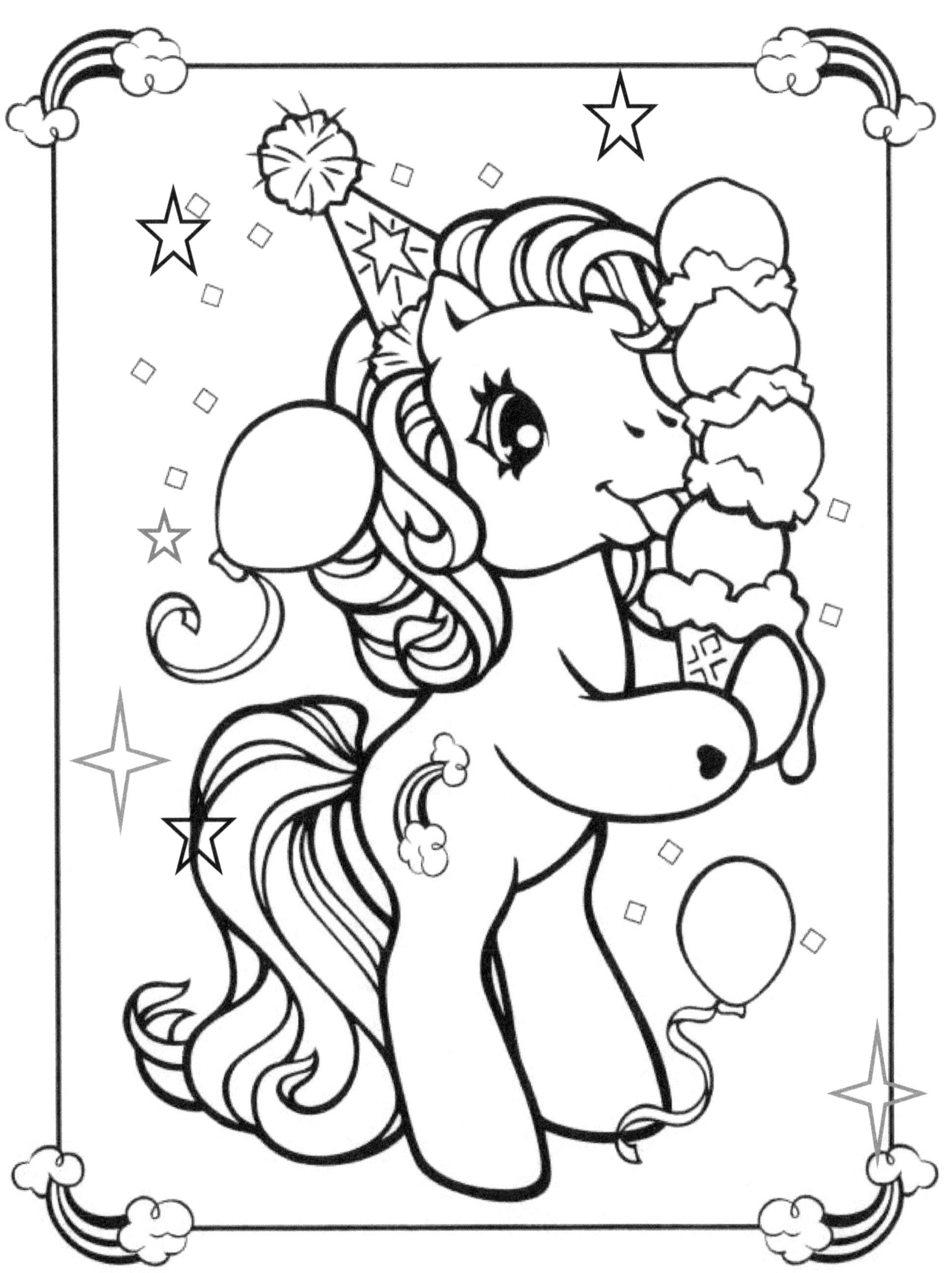

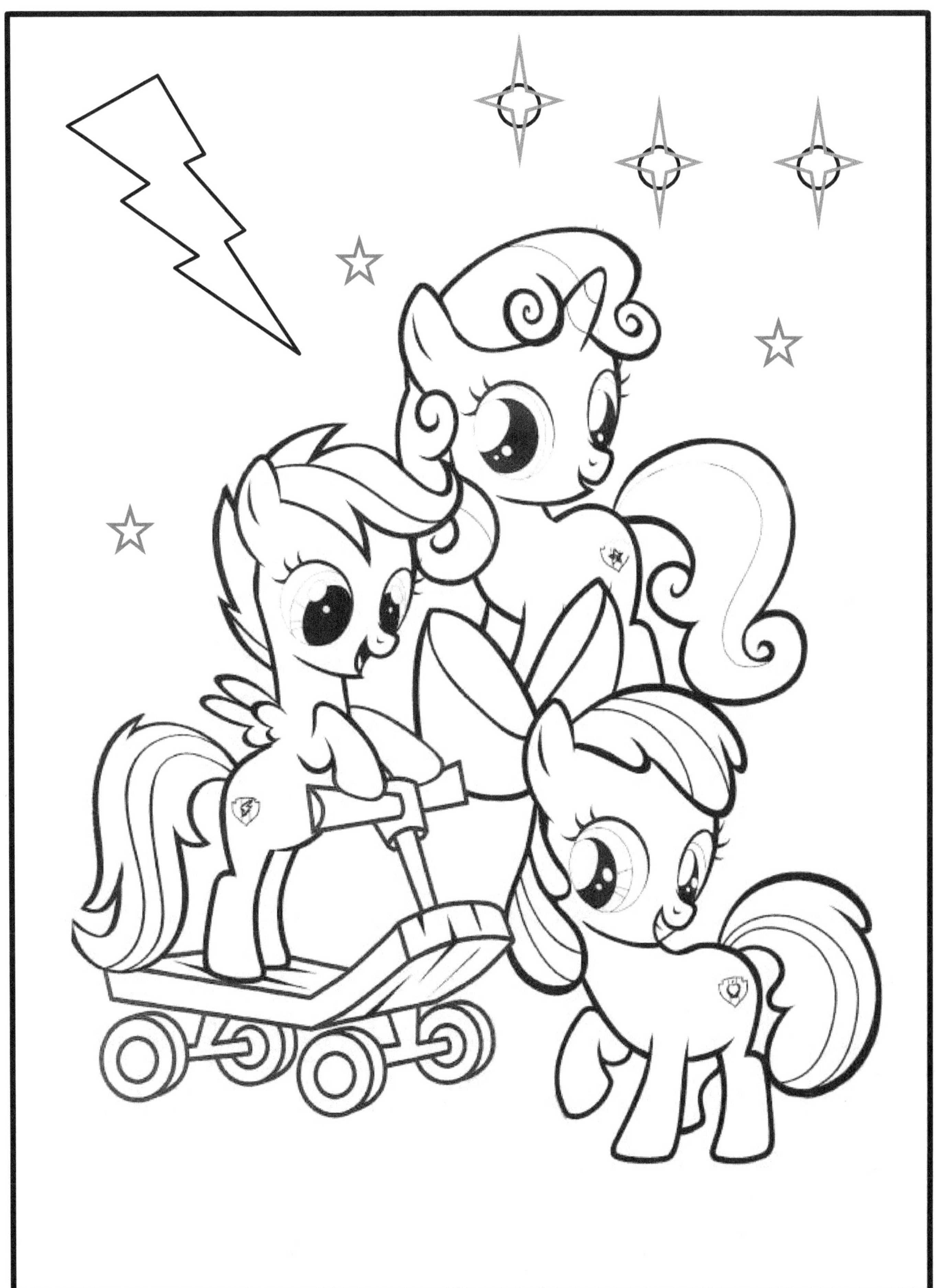

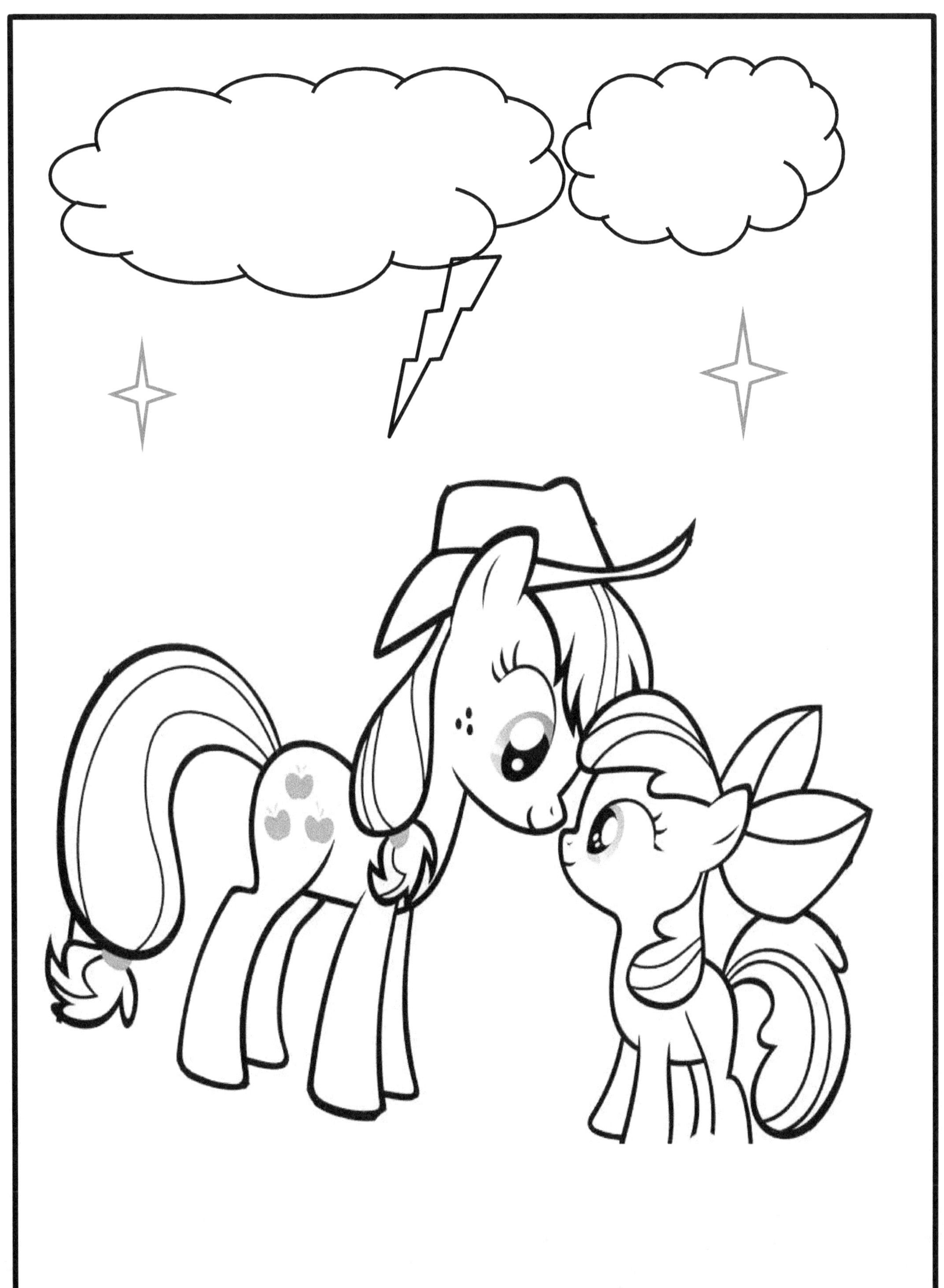

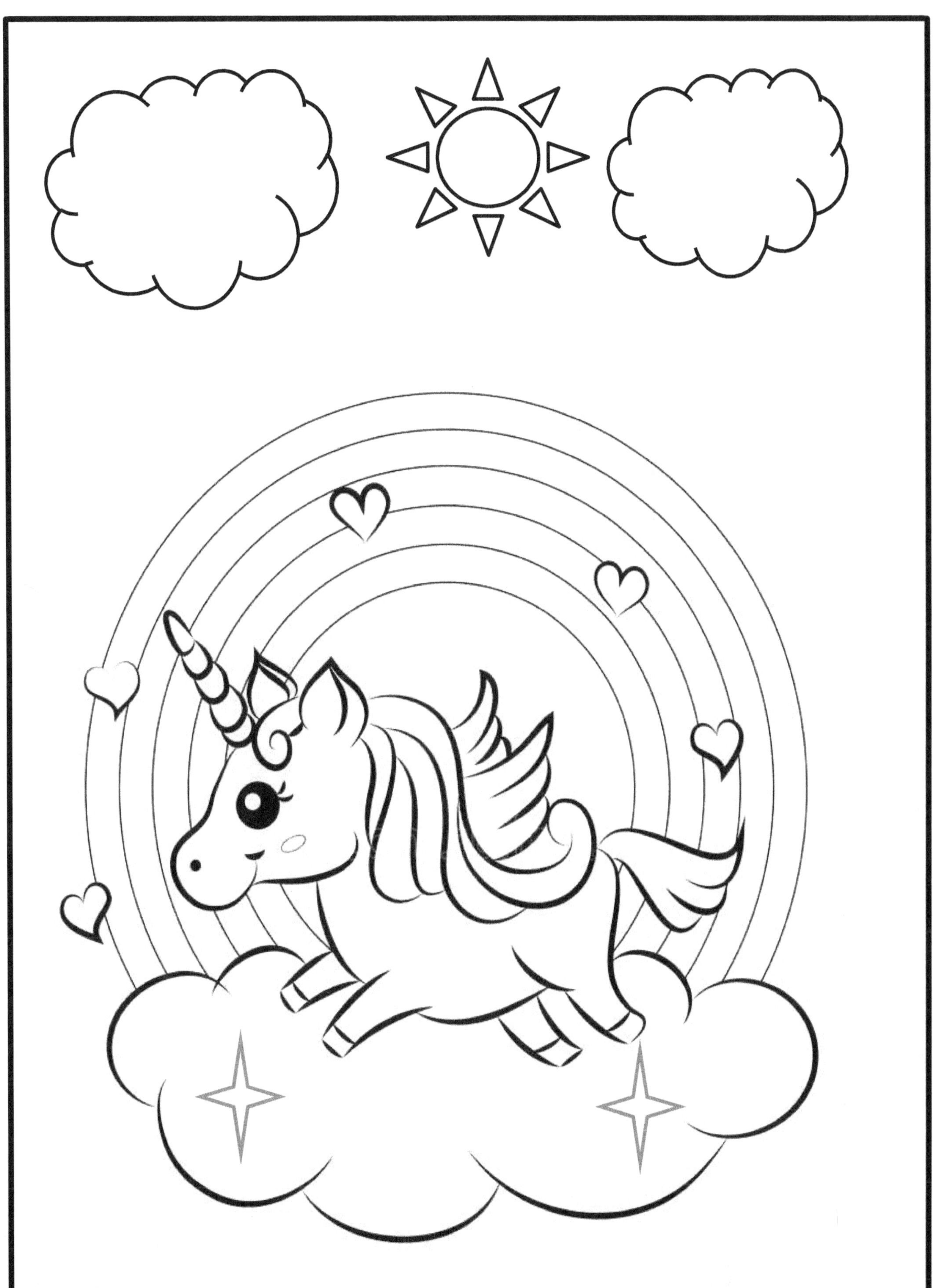

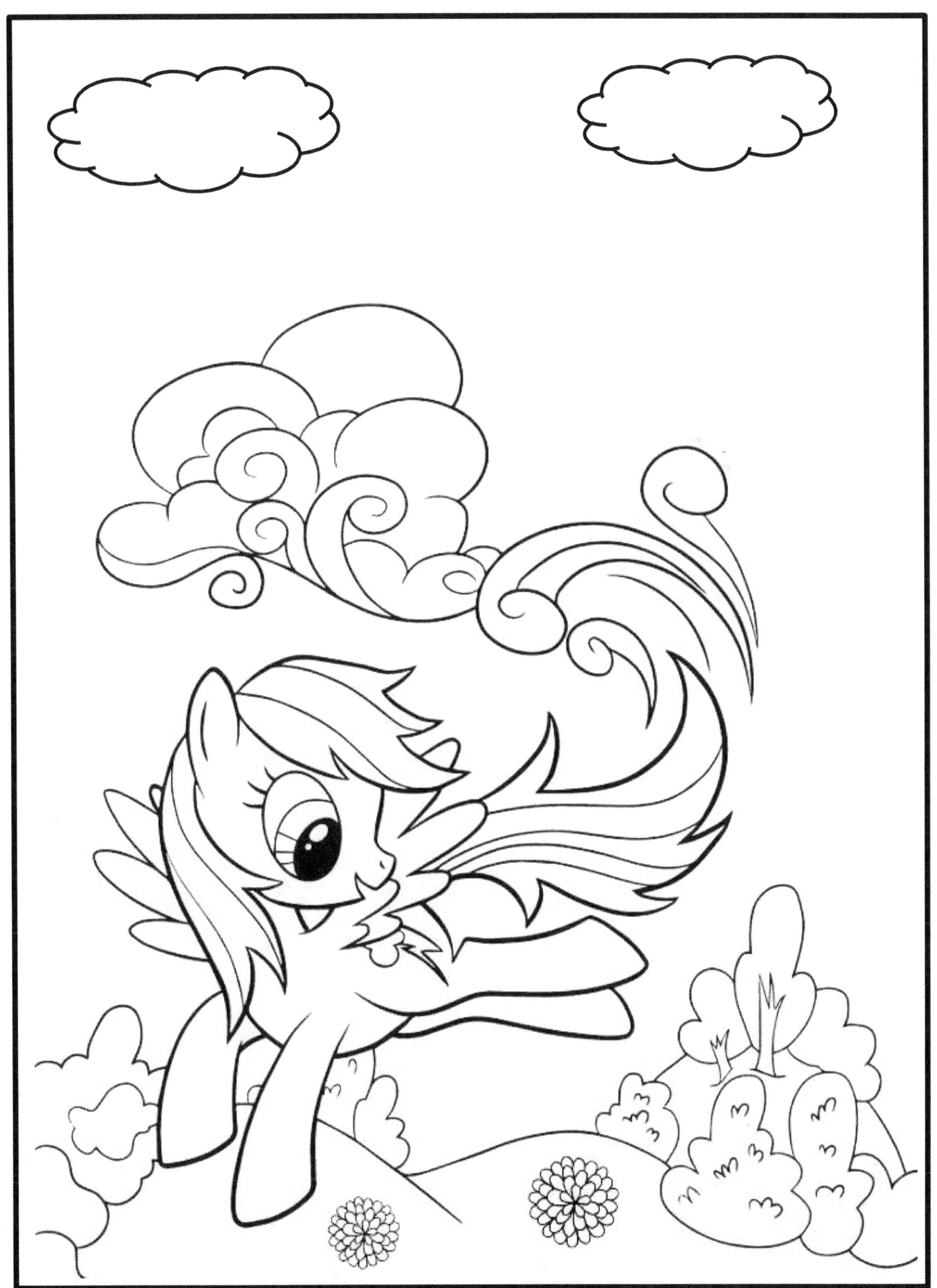

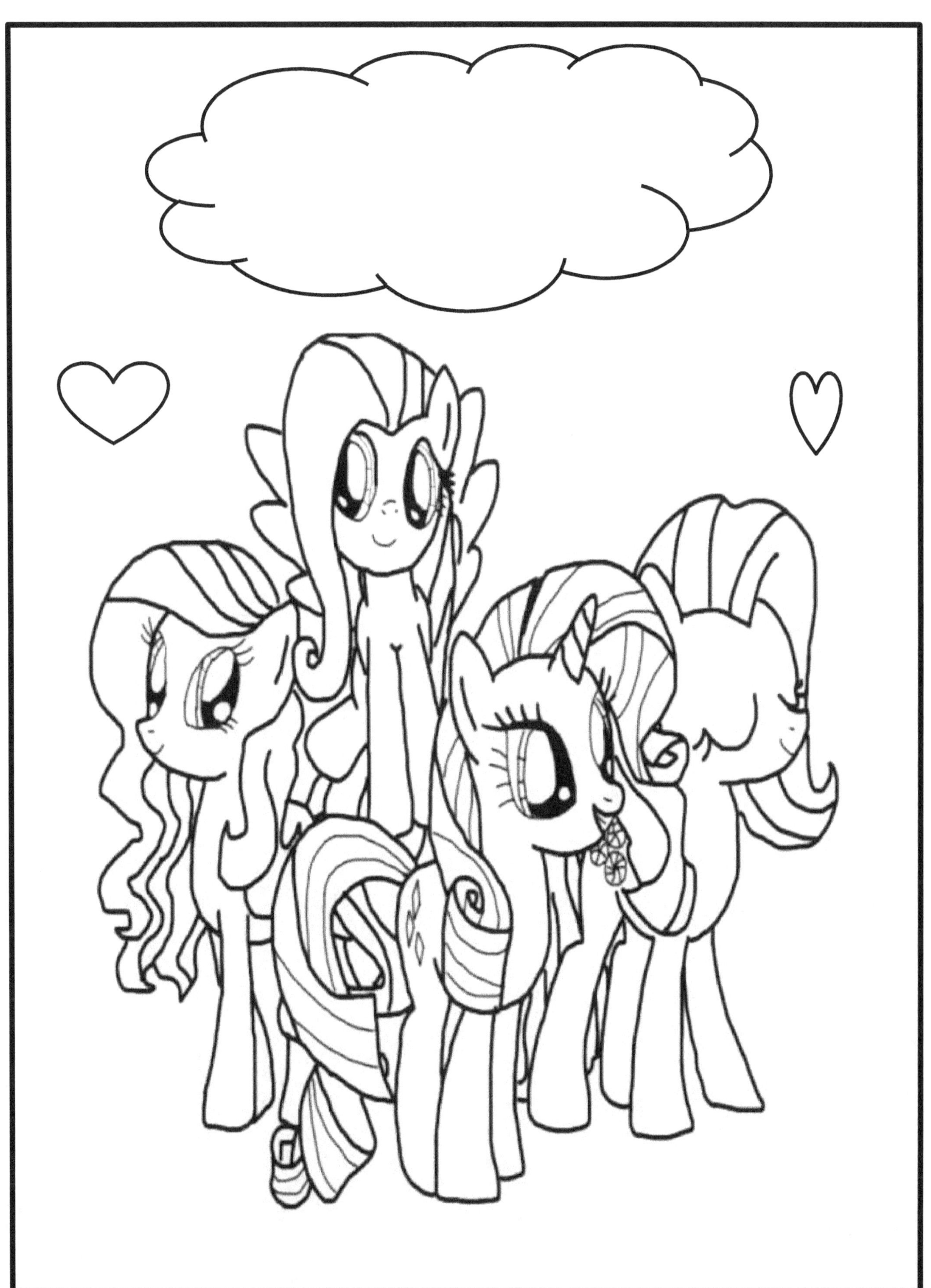

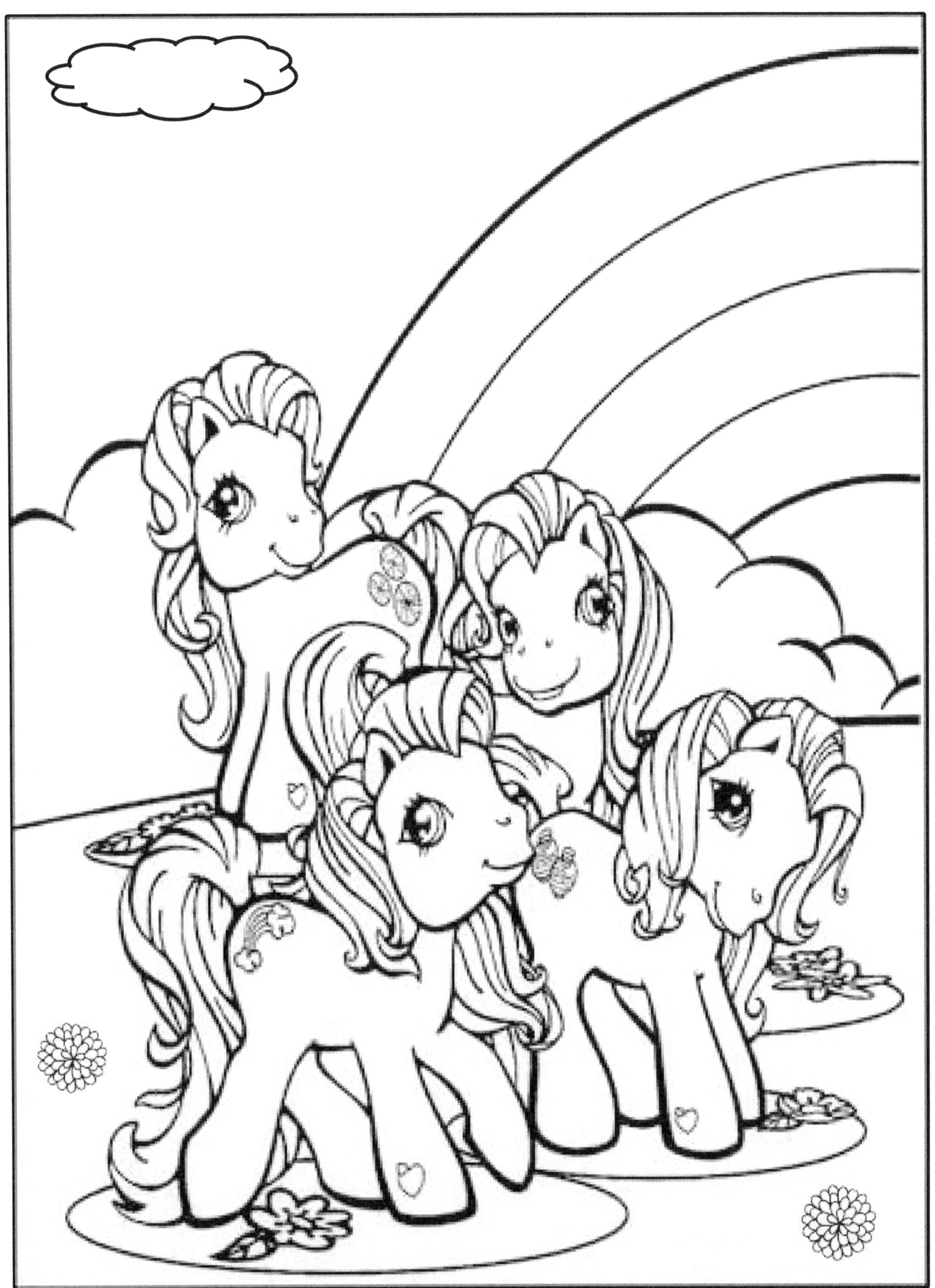

TEST COLORS